MONEY WISE AND SPIRITUALLY RICH

MONEY WISE AND SPIRITUALLY RICH

Dennis R. Deaton

BOOKCRAFT
Salt Lake City, Utah

Bookcraft is a registered trademark of Bookcraft, Inc.

Library of Congress Catalog Card Number: 98-71543

ISBN 1-57008-424-6

First Printing, 1998

Printed in the United States of America

To all the poor in spirit,
that they may
come unto Him.

CONTENTS

ACKNOWLEDGMENTS

I express my deepest appreciation to my daughter April Price who contributed much to the structure and content of the book—to my wife, Susan, who is my collaborator in all things—and to Sunshine Bird and Silvana Longone who added polish to the manuscript—and to the talented team at Bookcraft.

ONE

MINES OF SPIRITUAL
AND ETERNAL WEALTH

*It is our duty individually, as well as our privilege, to
learn how to dispose of the earthly wealth we may possess, to the glory of Him who has permitted us to hold it,
for in temporal blessings honestly obtained and wisely
placed to their legitimate use are concealed mines of spiritual and eternal wealth* (Brigham Young, *Journal of
Discourses*, 9:255; hereafter cited as *JD*).

To be rich by worldly weights or measures is not the goal.
The goal is to attain eternal life, for "he that hath eternal life is
rich" (D&C 6:7; 11:7). Those who would settle for the wealth of
the world at the expense of the wealth of eternity give themselves a monumental and everlasting booby prize. Indeed, the
quintessential test question on the mortality exam hinges on
making and maintaining that very distinction.

Yet money can be a remarkable schoolmaster. It can help
lead us to personal breakthroughs on the pathway to perfection
and to the rewards awaiting the honest and faithful. This book
intends to take the temporal subject of money and demystify it,
making it manageable and fruitful on an everyday earthly
plane. It teaches principles and procedures for solving and sur-
mounting many of life's most perplexing financial puzzles.
That alone would be significant, but this book intends to do
more. It is going to keep pointing you to a higher plane, invit-
ing you to see the eternal parallels and implications of your

monetary motions. It is not only going to teach you what to do and how to do it but also is going to have a lot to say about why.

While having a great deal of money is not necessarily a sign of God's favor, or the lack of it a sign of His disapproval, many of us should be much more successful with money than we are. We continue to suffer the consequences of a host of self-inflicted wounds. Learning how to properly manage what we have, whether meager or much, constitutes a major part of our test and triggers a good part of our growth.

As we learn and apply correct principles of money management we inevitably develop traits and characteristics that make us more fit for the kingdom of God. I do not think any of that is happenstantial. One of the unavoidable realities of mortality is how much of it bears on and is highly influenced by monetary operations. To my mind this unavoidably discloses God's hand in the matter.

Since the Father's plan of salvation has been meticulously designed for the express purpose of building and refining His offspring, and since He has made an incalculably enormous investment in this venture—not even withholding the life of His Only Begotten Son—the persistent dealings involving money must be, by divine design, a part of the curriculum we are to learn and master.

Practicing sound financial principles enhances not only our earth life but our eternal prospects as well. One cannot achieve and maintain wealth without eliminating procrastination from one's life, or without developing and practicing consistent levels of discipline, frugality, industry, delayed gratification, persistence, and thrift—a fairly laudable list of traits when you look at it. In summary, one cannot fully master money without developing mastery of oneself in the process.

You may not initially agree. You will point out that you have neighbors right and left who are undisciplined ingrates but who seem to have no end of cash and who live a lifestyle more ample than your own. Ah, my friend, this is where you must do as the Lord did with the sons of Jesse (see 1 Samuel 16:7). You must look beyond the outward appearance, for there are many who can keep up the *appearance* of wealth for a season but who will eventually and inevitably experience the fruits of their tactics and will reap a disappointing harvest for their charade.

One of the objectives of this book is to overthrow many of the prevalent myths and follies of our generation. Make no mistake about it—those who really do possess a great deal of cash and who are able to dispense it properly for the good of themselves and others have made some major strides in self-mastery. As the Prophet Joseph used to say, "Mark it down, Sidney."

So I extend to you a heartfelt invitation to become an earthly financial success on the way to achieving true and everlasting wealth—salvation in the eternal realms through Jesus Christ the Lord. As you apply the principles and methods outlined in this book, you will find yourself taking more and more personal responsibility for your monetary life and will see that your own character stands unrivaled as the crucial factor in your financial and spiritual quests.

The pathway to financial freedom is not arduous, back-breaking, or improbable. Neither is it a cake walk. If you have been struggling thus far, you will have to think new thoughts, make and keep new commitments, and stiffen your backbone a bit. All of that brings more than ample rewards. Financial freedom is not easy, but it is definitely worth the effort, for its rewards are of temporal *and* spiritual consequence. When the path is properly pursued, the Spirit will guide your feet virtually every step of the way and you will become increasingly aware of the Lord's personal love for you.

With that blessed knowledge growing inside, you will gain greater desires to grow and to master your appetites and passions. You will develop an increased awe and respect for Him who guides and supports you, and who has trod the path before you with perfection. You will come to realize that your dependence upon Him must not stem from a self-indulgent lack of effort but from the need for His enabling grace and strength to see and do what it takes to succeed. As you do all in your power, He will supply you with whatever else may be needed to accomplish the goal. Gaining confidence in the law of grace, you will understand what it takes to *fully live* the first principles and ordinances of the gospel in such a way as to *fully receive* the blessings promised to the faithful.

TWO

IRREVOCABLE LAWS

I, the Lord, am bound when ye do what I say; but when ye do not what I say, ye have no promise (D&C 82:10).

As you read this book, sooner or later you are going to ask, "Who is Dennis Deaton, and why does he have any right to be telling me anything about money? I wonder if he lives this stuff himself, or if he's just another do-as-I-say-and-not-as-I-do guy hawking a book."

Let me save you some time, so you can quickly make up your mind whether you want to read this book or move to the Louis L'Amour section of the bookstore, where you'll *know* what you're reading is fiction.

Here's what I'm not: I am not the richest man in the world or even in the Church. I may not even be the richest high priest in my ward. (I live in a fairly affluent ward and I don't go around checking net worths at the ward socials.) I am not a professor of finance, economics, or accounting. (Perhaps that hits you as a plus—this book may actually be *fun to read* as well as insightful.) I am not a General Authority. Not too impressive so far, I agree, and here's another thing: I also do not claim to know all there is to know about money. Undoubtedly, I have gallons more to learn, but if I waited until I learned it all before I wrote a book I would never get around to sharing with you the truly priceless things I have learned already.

Here's what I *am*: a lifelong member of the Church, with a testimony of the latter-day work. I worship the Father in the name of the Son, Jesus Christ, and diligently seek to repent and bring forth fruit meet for repentance. (This book is one such effort.) Every day I strive to "always remember Him" and to put Him before any idol or earthly pursuit. My greatest joy and satisfaction come when I feel the closeness of His Spirit as I live the living gospel. I revere the teachings of the Prophet Joseph Smith and the other prophets and Apostles of this dispensation. I have a personal goal to spend more time each week reading or listening to the scriptures and the words of the Brethren than reading, watching, or listening to the world—television, news broadcasts, financial reports and commentary, sports events, or movies.

Finally, I am a father of nine children (which proves that I'm either insane or have a strong mind and a reasonably active sense of humor), a new grandfather of one great little boy (who's smarter than any of your kids or grandkids), and have been married to the same wonderful queen-of-a-woman for over twenty-seven years (which perhaps suggests that *her* sanity is suspect).

Key to my perspectives about money stands the truth that I have been at one time in my life in ugly financial straits. I know the pain and distress of having bill collectors send nasty letters, of threats on the phone, and of attorneys rattling the sabers of bankruptcy and foreclosure. Through the Lord's blessings, guidance, and help I have climbed out of that pit and in the process have gained extremely valuable insights about money on both temporal and spiritual planes. So let me share for now a small part of my experience, the part that set the stage for the writing of this book.

As a married man and father with a good profession and a good income, I sought to increase my financial strength. My intentions were worthy enough, I suppose, but I made some huge blunders. The first one was very subtle. Only in retrospect did I realize what a mistake it was.

My financial misery began when I chose to disobey the counsel of Alma: "Trust no one to be your teacher . . . except he be a man of God, walking in his ways and keeping his commandments" (Mosiah 23:14). I began reading some of the highly touted, best-seller books on "financial success" and followed them.

Before long I noticed something was amiss. Rather than my growing suddenly rich, my cash flow and net worth were going south like a flock of mallards in a September cold snap. Before I could throw the brakes on this cableless elevator, I was mired in a quagmire of debt, lousy "investments," and insufficient cash flow.

The ensuing months were a nightmare. The specters grew even worse as the months became years. Needless to say, I prayed. Over a year went by with my praying the same prayer—"Save me, Lord, save me." I spent many sleepless nights trying to sort out the mess, but nothing seemed to help. The misery grew worse as our financial plight deepened. As losing everything we had ever worked for became a real possibility, my prayers intensified. "Save me, Lord! Thou hast all power in heaven and on earth. If thou wilt, thou canst make me whole. Please save me!"

With everything going down the drain—my self-esteem, our home, and, worst of all, our word in keeping commitments and obligations to our fellowmen—I at long last broke through and received the answer I so sorely needed.

There came no windfall out of the blue. Ed McMahon did not personally present me with a check; I did not at the last moment receive an unexpected inheritance from a long-lost relative, nor did my creditors suddenly forgive my debts. Something infinitely more valuable came. The Lord spoke to my mind a simple sentence. I'd heard it before. Many times. In fact I had already had it memorized and had used it in myriad talks and lessons. But it hit me like a thunderbolt, and my whole soul reverberated with the understanding.

"Dennis, 'there is a law irrevocably decreed in heaven before the foundations of this world, upon which *all* blessings are predicated—and when we obtain any blessing from God, it is by obedience to that law upon which it is predicated' (D&C 130:20; emphasis added)". In one electric moment, I understood that I had been praying wrong! All these months I'd been asking for the Lord to do it all. I'd been pleading (and quite intensely, too) for the Lord to provide "instant salvation" as though He were some kind of a genie and all I needed to do was to close my eyes, rub the lamp, and wish really hard. And the Lord just doesn't work that way.

The Father and the Son are engaged in the work of "bring[ing] to pass the immortality and eternal life of man" (Moses 1:39). Everything they do furthers that work. At no time will they do anything to undermine that divine purpose. Granting instant salvation to slothful and unwise servants would be totally inconsistent with the plan. They will not do it. Doing so would only weaken the weak. They are in the business of raising up strong, righteous, humbly self-reliant sons and daughters.

I knew all this. Why had it taken me so long to see and do it? From that moment forward the words of my prayers demonstrated a radical change. They went a little more like this: "Dear Heavenly Father, please help me to learn and understand the laws and principles of financial salvation, and please Lord, help me gain the strength to obey them."

When I began praying that prayer my whole universe shifted. The clouds of gloom and doom parted and the rays of hope shone through again. Line upon line and precept upon precept, as I learned and applied the principles, my financial kingdom went surely and steadily from rags to riches.

My financial odyssey has turned out to be a priceless journey rife with insights and treasures. I have gained incredibly valuable perspectives and (dare I say it?) revelations about money and our mortal journey back to the presence of God. The principles, as all eternal principles do, apply to both the temporal and the spiritual realms and cast celestial light on how we can be good and faithful stewards in both kingdoms. They are so monumentally significant, so enlightening and effective, that I can't wait to share them with you.

THREE

LESSONS IN STEWARDSHIP

Wherefore, verily I say unto you that all things unto me are spiritual, and not at any time have I given unto you a law which was temporal; neither any man, nor the children of men; neither Adam, your father, whom I created" (D&C 29:34).

Joseph Smith declared, "It is impossible for a man to be saved in ignorance" (D&C 131:6). As Latter-day Saints we heartily accept that truth, yet mostly we do so without challenging our minds by asking "What type of ignorance?" or "Ignorance of what?" Those of us who frequently quote the Prophet tend to think that he was referring to some body of information—a certain set of facts to store in our minds. We more or less automatically assume that Joseph was exhorting us to improve our academic database about the doctrines of the kingdom. And in my opinion he certainly was, for we have a great need to expand what we know about the doctrines, laws, and covenants. But that is only the beginning—a prelude—of the ignorance he wants us to vanquish.

While we do not know how long we lived and developed as spirits in the premortal life, it seems probable that before the veil was drawn, we knew more than we know now. We have forgotten all that knowledge, of course. Perhaps much of our academic learning in this life amounts to *recovery* rather than *discovery*. Depending upon individual diligence in that prior life, there may be locked away somewhere in many souls a veritable library of information that they cannot currently access. Yet that obviously was not enough. When many were basking in all that knowledge all of us were still ignorant in one very important area. We did not have the knowledge and skill of how to apply that knowledge and govern a physical body to practice and live according to that knowledge.

It is like riding a bike. We could take a class on bicycle riding from Greg LeMond, someone who really knows the subject. Greg could stand at a chalkboard and make sketches and write statements, all of which could flow into our notes. We could go on field trips, observing others riding bikes. We could view hours of video with live shots, animation, and slow-motion segments. We could receive countless quantities of descriptions, diagrams, and dialogue, filling our intellects with reams of material on the art of riding a bike, yet we would still be ignorant. We would still not *know how* to ride a bike.

We can only overcome *that* level of ignorance by living the experience ourselves. Each of us must get a bicycle, mount it, and try riding the thing. As we endeavor to apply the intellectual ideas, we really grasp their meaning. We really *get* what the instructor was saying. When that "magical" moment comes—the moment when we actually "get the feel" of balance and control and can really ride the bike—we have enlightenment. We break through the veil of ignorance, bursting into the bright rays of full knowledge and understanding. And what a great feeling it is when we go from intellectual or academic knowledge to the pure joy of practical know-how!

Make no mistake about it, the quest for eternal life and exaltation involves academic excellence, intellectual effort, and tireless scholarship; and it goes beyond. The test we must pass is not oral or written. It is a no-nonsense practical exam.

In one of the Prophet Joseph Smith's early epistles he eloquently and clearly drew the distinction between acquiring knowledge and practicing it, the difference between hearing and obeying:

> It is necessary for men to receive an understanding concerning the laws of the heavenly kingdom, before they are permitted to enter it . . . But when this fact is admitted, that the immediate will of heaven is contained in the Scriptures, are we not

bound as rational creatures to live in accordance to all its precepts? Will the mere admission, that this is the will of heaven
ever benefit us if we do not comply with all its teachings? . . .
[His] rest is of such perfection and glory, that man has need of
a preparation before he can, according to the laws of that kingdom, enter it and enjoy its blessings. This being the fact, God
has given certain laws to the human family, which, if
observed, are sufficient to prepare them to inherit his rest.
(*Teachings of the Prophet Joseph Smith*, comp. Joseph Fielding
Smith [Salt Lake City: Deseret Book, 1976], pp. 51-54; hereafter
cited as *TPJS*.)

LEARNING FROM THE CHILDREN OF THIS WORLD

Recorded in the Gospel of Luke (16:1–12) is one of the
Lord's most provocative parables: "And he said also *unto his
disciples,* There was a certain rich man, which had a steward;
and the same was accused unto him that he had wasted his
goods" (vs. 1). Please note that Jesus directs this parable to
those who have chosen to follow him. Not to the Pharisees. Not
to the Sadducees. Not to the Gentiles. Not to unbelievers, but
to his disciples and those who wish to be.

"And he called him, and said unto him, How is it that I
hear this of thee? give an account of thy stewardship; for thou
mayest be no longer steward" (vs. 2).

The rich man sets an appointment for a stewardship interview, based on some accusations of misuse of his assets on the
part of his steward. Apparently the steward is in fact guilty, for
he makes no effort to mount a defense. Instead he plots an exit
strategy, which actually compounds his transgressions against
his current employer. While still the lord's steward, he goes to
each of his lord's debtors and falsifies the ledgers in their favor.
Evidently he has no compunctions about committing further
fraud. His sole interest now is to prepare for his future. He
seeks at whatever moral cost to buy the debtors' good will so
that, when he is expelled from his present position, he may be
able to find favor with them. The provocative twist to all of this
is that the unjust steward receives commendation for his tactics.

"And the lord commended the unjust steward, because he had done wisely: for the children of this world are in their generation wiser than the children of light" (vs. 8).

Obviously, the unjust steward is not commended for his unlawful or dishonest acts. They speak for themselves and are far from praiseworthy. However, there remains one aspect of the steward's actions that on a temporal plane demonstrates wisdom, and Jesus points to that one aspect in order to jolt some of his disciples—the children of light—out of their spiritual complacency. Praising a cheat would shock the Lord's flock and perhaps wake them up.

The unjust steward was indeed wise in one key respect, albeit on the short-lived, temporal level only. What was that wisdom? The unjust steward was actively engaged in preparing for his future! He wanted to end up in favorable circumstances and he was going to do everything in his power to ensure it. He is not taking his future state for granted or leaving anything to chance. He was in action, doing what he needed to do to prepare for the "life to come." In that respect he was wise.

Are we who claim to be the children of light that wise? Are we exhibiting that same level of all-out commitment to prepare in this life for the everlasting realms ahead? Do we apply, in a righteous way, the same total, no-sacrifice-is-too-great attitude to our celestial quest? Aren't we Latter-day Saints a bit lazy, thinking that modest efforts here and there will suffice?

Note Elder Wilford Woodruff's comment: "I ask, in the name of God and humanity, why is it that intelligent beings, made in the image of God, take no interest in their condition after death? They know they are going to die, and, if they have any sense or reflection, they know they will live after the death of their mortal bodies; still men will sell their eternal interest for money, for a few hundred or a few thousand dollars they will sell all the interest they have in the eternal world; in fact, they take no interest in their eternal welfare." (JD, 18:34–35.)

God *will* take care of us, and we *do not* work our way to heaven. We are saved by grace. But that grace is allocated in accordance with a divinely just system wherein we must be engaged in doing all that is in our power. As we do so, the grace and power of our Lord and Savior Jesus Christ will be extended to us, and through His merits and mercy we will be saved.

The question remains for each of us to answer in his own heart. Do we put forth our utmost efforts, or do we do just enough to look good to the rest of the ward? Many of "the children of this world"—those who have no faith in a life hereafter, and have, as far as they are concerned, only this life to live—exert greater diligence in preparing for *that* future than do many of us who hold loftier and more accurate views of the plan. Who then is the more foolish? Who exhibits the greater wisdom?

After you have pondered those probing questions for a while, look at what else the Savior had to say on this occasion: "And I say unto you, Make to yourselves friends of [and D&C 82:22 says 'with' rather than 'of'] the mammon of unrighteousness; that, when ye fail, they may receive you into everlasting habitations" (Luke 16:9).

Is not the Lord Jesus Christ teaching His disciples that their place in the everlasting habitations will at least in part be predicated on how well they manage their stewardship over the temporal resources with which they are entrusted? "All that we possess of this world's goods has been given to us of the Lord, and we are to be regarded as but stewards over what we have received. We will have to give an accounting for our stewardship." (Elder George F. Richards, Conference Report, April 1948, p.19; hereafter cited as CR.)

If we use our resources wisely—our talents, time, money, and assets—for the building up of the kingdom, it will be well with us. When we fail, that is, when our mortal tenements fail and we die, if we have made friends of eternal beings through the righteous use of our "mammon of unrighteousness," they, the Eternal Gods, will receive us into everlasting habitations.

> He that is faithful in that which is least is faithful also in much: and he that is unjust in the least is unjust also in much.
> If therefore ye have not been faithful in the unrighteous mammon, who will commit to your trust the true riches?

And if ye have not been faithful in that which is another man's, who shall give you that which is your own? (Luke 16:10-12.)

 How sound and penetrating this logic! Does it not border on the preposterous for us to think that we might be entrusted with the endless resources of eternity and the full powers of the priesthood when we cannot even live within a budget? Can we ever hope to organize matter into worlds and govern them if we cannot even govern our checkbook? Can we expect to attain spiritual salvation when we cannot attain temporal salvation?

 Brigham Young observed, "It is to our advantage to take good care of the blessings God bestows upon us; if we pursue the opposite course, we cut off the power and glory God designs we should inherit" (*JD*, 9:171).

Even more pointedly, Elder Bruce R. McConkie declared:

Work is the law of life: it is the ruling principle in the lives of the Saints. We cannot, while physically able, voluntarily shift the burden of our own support to others. Doles abound in evils. Industry, thrift, and self-respect are essential to salvation. We must maintain our own health, sow our own gardens, store our own food, educate and train ourselves to handle the daily affairs of life. No one else can work out our salvation for us, either temporally or spiritually. (*Ensign*, May 1979, p. 93.)

Every minute of every day our stewardship skills are on display, and we are being tested and judged by how well we develop and utilize them. Assuming we are striving to live a righteous life, to decide whether we are ready for our stewardship interview with our Lord we need look no further than our own household affairs.

FOUR

PATTERNS OF SALVATION

Built . . . into the seemingly ordinary experiences of life are abundant opportunities for us to acquire the eternal attributes (Neal A. Maxwell, *We Will Prove Them Herewith* [Salt Lake City: Deseret Book, 1982], p. 11).

God gives us laws on many levels. Again, as with learning to ride a bike, sometimes He offers us "training wheels." The scriptures teach that Elias must first come and restore us to straight paths, the lesser light pointing the way and leading us to the greater light. There is no salvation in the lesser or preparatory laws, only in the higher. Nevertheless we may and must learn to practice the lesser laws in order to gain the wisdom and strength to understand and know how to practice the higher.

The dealings with money and earthly wealth systems, which we can hardly avoid or evade in mortality (even though we sometimes wish we could), in essence constitute an "Elias," which Father uses as a schoolmaster to lead us to higher planes. As we seek to achieve some degree of financial "salvation," we come to learn about the divine balance between works and grace, so crucial to our *spiritual* salvation. We come to understand what dependence upon the Lord means and what it doesn't mean. We come to understand the delicate distinction between the type of self-reliance the Lord wants us to develop and the type of arrogant self-sufficiency that affronts Him.

Furthermore, He uses these preparatory systems to instruct and edify *all of His children*. His love being so perfect and His work so vast, His plan comprehends and includes all mankind without discrimination or respect of persons. The Apostle Peter declared, "But in every nation he that feareth him, and worketh righteousness, is accepted with him" (Acts 10:35). Thus we may be sure that anyone who obeys correct laws and principles, on whatever level, will not lose his reward. They will receive blessings commensurate with the level of law they are obeying, and in proportion to the heed and diligence they render. Members of The Church of Jesus Christ of Latter-day Saints or not, God's children receive according to their <u>works and desires.</u>

SOLID RESEARCH

Thus we can learn a great deal from those who have achieved genuine success in their temporal affairs. However, we must be careful to distinguish between authentic, solid success and that which merely perpetrates the facade of success. Two reputable research studies on how the wealthy become wealthy can serve us. These findings are so consistent with one another that they merit our careful consideration.

The first study was published in the early 1980s. Funded in part by the National Science Foundation, the study monitored fifteen hundred middle-class Americans for a twenty-year period, from 1960 to 1980. In addition, interviews were conducted with two hundred millionaires, among whom were some fairly famous names. Norman Lear, Lee Iacocca, and Jane Cahill Pfeiffer were but a few of the financial elite who were interviewed in the study.

More recently (1996), and even more impressively, a more extensive study was conducted by two Ph.Ds, Thomas Stanley and William Danko, on precisely the same topic—how rich people get to be rich. They conducted in-depth surveys with over eleven thousand high-income earners and more than five hundred multimillionaires. (The average net worth of the multimillionaires was over $3.5 million.) It is remarkable that the findings of both studies are so similar and so concordant with the teachings of our Church leaders and the wisdom of the ages that one cannot ignore their conclusions nor the conspicuous "pattern of salvation" they depict.

These studies not only show a pattern for gaining and managing temporal wealth but also demonstrate that the eternal significance of these "training wheels" cannot be underestimated. Embedded in the wonderful, practical counsel they give us lie higher doctrines of immense value.

Here is the sum and substance of the studies:

MULTIMILLIONAIRES SELF-MADE, SELF-SUSTAINING

As a rule, wealthy people are conspicuously self-reliant individuals. They work and sacrifice for their success, placing independence high on their list of values. Eighty percent of the multimillionaires made their fortune in one generation. Dependants they are not! They stand on their own feet, unweakened by doles, gifts, or lavish inheritances from their kin. Fewer than 25 percent were given more than $10,000 by their parents. More than half never received so much as one solitary dollar by way of inheritance. And how many received a big chunk of the family business as a gift? Nine percent.

Multimillionaires also tend to be well educated, but with one added distinction: the majority put themselves through college. Nearly half of these did it all, having paid every penny of their tuition and expenses. It is quite apparent that a crucial part of their education came outside the formal classroom. Skills in discipline, sacrifice, time management, and financial prudence cannot be imparted by a professor. Such skills are obtained by exercise and practice. Taking full responsibility for themselves, these financial high achievers discovered *their own value* and developed solid confidence in their ability to compete and succeed in the real world. (Hey, Mona, what do you think of canceling Bobby's credit cards at BYU?)

SELF-SUSTAINING SAINTS

President Brigham Young repeatedly taught the doctrine: "We want you henceforth to be a self-sustaining people. Hear it, O Israel! hear it neighbors, friends and enemies, this is what the Lord requires of this people." (*JD*, 12:285.)

Heavenly Father, as any loving father does, rejoices in the growth and development of His children. Although we cherish our helpless infants, and love to cuddle and caress them, their utter dependency upon us is not their intended end or destiny. They grow daily on an inexorable course en route to becoming full-fledged, self-governing adults, replicating the works of their parents. On this earth there is no pattern more plain or more often repeated than that one. No living creature on this planet has been designed to be an eternal dependant on its parent. Quite the contrary. So for us the goal is righteous independence.

Thus it should be clear to all that God's purpose lies in schooling and guiding each one of us on the astounding journey from a state of utter, total dependence to the glorious state of being, in all respects, as perfect, as powerful and as righteously independent as He. The Prophet Joseph Smith taught us:

> Here, then, is eternal life—to know the only wise and true God; and you have *got to learn how to be Gods* yourselves . . . the same as all Gods have done before you, namely, by going from one small degree to another, and from a small capacity to a great one. . . . God himself, finding he was in the midst of spirits and glory, because he was more intelligent, saw proper to institute laws whereby the rest could have a privilege to advance like himself. (*TPJS*, pp. 346, 354; emphasis added.)

It appears, then, that godhood is not simply awarded or conferred; it has to be developed. Our responsibility (and how glorious a thought!) amounts to learning how to live the same principles to the same perfect degree as our eternal parents. The Father and the Son want us to understand that we *can* depend on them, not that forevermore we *must* depend on them.

Keep in mind that in Lehi's dream the sojourners had to grasp the iron rod and hand over hand move their way up the path in order to enjoy the full sweetness of God's love and the fruits of eternal life. There was no catering service.

BE FRUGAL AND UNPRETENTIOUS

Contrary to the cherished stereotype, the vast majority of multimillionaires are very frugal, unassuming people. They are *not* conspicuous in their consumption. Far from it.

Most millionaires do not live in opulent mansions. They dwell in modest homes and drive fairly conservative cars. Occasionally you can find a Porsche or a Ferrari parked in their garage but, guess what! Those are owned by the minority group of millionaires who inherited their wealth. The ones who earned their wealth thought that anyone who bought a Maserati should not be granted a driver's license (insane people should not be allowed to drive, you know) and anyone who bought a *second* Jaguar exhibited a pronounced learning disability.

On the wrists of self-made millionaires you do not find a gaudy Rolex. Consumption like that is totally out of character for them. "Why would you pay that much for something that just tells time?" they query. "A good ninety-dollar Seiko works just as well." They snicker and shake their heads at people who shell out big bucks for something that merely feeds their ego. (Hey, Marge, do you think we have enough Grey Poupon in our food storage?)

By contrast, people with high incomes but low net worth exhibit two opposite tendencies: (1) They rate high on the consumption scale, and (2) They pay a lot of interest. Our modern studies corroborate what wise folks have been saying and doing all along. Francis Wayland said: "Wealth is not acquired, as many persons suppose, by fortunate speculations and splendid enterprises, but the daily practice of industry, frugality and economy. He who relies upon these means will rarely be found destitute, and he who relies upon any other, will generally become bankrupt." ("Thoughts on the Business Life," *Forbes*, 13 April 1981, p. 212.)

If you are from North Carolina you have a commendable state motto: "To be, rather than seem." Multimillionaires live that philosophy. They want to *be* rich rather than merely *appear to be* rich.

USE DEBT SPARINGLY IF AT ALL

Research on multimillionaires shows that they pay little or no interest, while those who generate big incomes but have little to show for it pay lots of interest. They are in debt and often deceive themselves into thinking that debt is actually a shrewd financial tactic to expand their kingdom. "Dumb," say the millionaires.

"Well, sure," someone might say, "they can pay cash for their cars—what do you expect? They're *millionaires!*" The point here is not to mistake which is the cause and which is the effect. So let me be clear. One of the major reasons why they achieve wealth is that they *gained* interest instead of paying it. They lived on the correct side of the interest equation and did not squander their earnings on unproductive expenditures like interest and finance charges. That's not *because* they are millionaires, that is *how they got to be* millionaires. Most of them own their homes outright, pay cash for their cars, and add to their wealth daily because early on they kicked the debt and deficit-spending addiction that plagues our society.

Debt is bondage. I did not invent the metaphor, the Lord did (see D&C 19:35). A clear and prevalent counsel throughout this entire gospel dispensation has been to stay away from this tyrannical parasite that siphons your wealth. I could share hundreds of admonitions from the Brethren. One will suffice. It's a classic:

> Interest never sleeps nor sickens nor dies; it never goes to the hospital; it works on Sundays and holidays; it never takes a vacation . . . it is never laid off work nor discharged from employment; it never works on reduced hours . . . it has no love, no sympathy; it is as hard and soulless as a granite cliff. Once in debt, interest is your companion every minute of the day and night; you cannot shun it or slip away from it; you cannot dismiss it; it yields neither to entreaties, demands, or

orders; and whenever you get in its way or cross its course or fail to meet its demands, it crushes you. (J. Reuben Clark, CR, April 1938, pp. 102-3.)

LOVE YOUR LIFE'S WORK

Many people look at their work as drudgery and a burden, something they wish they could escape. They yearn for 6:00 P.M. to roll around so they can head for home. They see their job as a temporary and annoying "necessary evil" that they dream of escaping as soon as possible. "As soon as I hit it big in the lottery, or as soon as my investments pay off, I'm going to quit this rat race and do something really meaningful with my life"—this dominates their thinking. Such "escapist" attitudes do not produce wealth because they circumvent service, which is one of the major lessons to learn in mortality. Even on temporal levels, those who "lose their life" in doing some form of good for their fellowmen wind up with a form of salvation.

People who become wealthy love what they do. They are not "just passing through." They have a talent they wish to express, or a service to render, or a product that benefits their fellowmen, and they love sharing that talent, service, or product with as many people as possible. They look at their life's work as one of their main purposes for being. Almost without exception (and long after they have enough money to live on for the rest of their life) financial high achievers continue doing what they are doing. Their work is more fun and satisfying to them than play. George Burns, in his mid-nineties, said: "Retire? Why would I want to retire? I love what I do. Besides, I'm booked at Carnegie Hall on my hundredth birthday. I can't quit or die now. I'd lose too much money."

Notice this summary from the National Science Foundation Study:

We originally expected the people in our sample to become wealthy through investing in . . . stocks, bonds and real estate. We anticipated that the wealthier someone became, the more of an amateur stock or real estate broker they'd become. It didn't work out that way. Rarely did they buy the most profitable stocks or buildings. In fact, their investment results were remarkably mediocre.

The actual source of their wealth was their work. In case after case, they did increasingly well occupationally, while their pursuit of investment profits proved to be largely a waste of time. In the long run, it was their work—and only their work—which made them rich. (Srully Blotnick, *Getting Rich Your Own Way* [New York: Doubleday & Co., Inc., 1980], p. 8.)

If you don't love work, and specifically your own life's work, it is highly unlikely that you will ever be a big financial success. You are going to struggle until you learn that life is about service and giving value to other people. People who only work until they get enough money so they can spend the rest of their days at the beach miss this one key truth: The Lord wants us to overcome selfishness and discover the vast joys of service. He wants us to lose our life in the building of others.

INVESTORS BUT NOT GAMBLERS

The pathway to riches is one of steadiness, not suddenness. The wealthy do not become rich overnight; they do, however, get rich surely and steadily. Unexpected windfalls and fortuitous landslides of cash are rare exceptions, and financial high achievers waste no time yearning for them. They set themselves a course and get after it. "Getting rich quick" plays absolutely no part in their thinking. Intuitively, they follow Ben Franklin's timeless wisdom: "I resolve to apply myself industriously to whatever business I take in hand, and not divert my mind from my business by any foolish project of growing suddenly rich; for industry and patience are the surest means to plenty."

When it comes to investing, millionaires get rich by harnessing time, not timing. Their investment plans are fairly conservative in general, characterized by stability and infrequent trades. They are not impatient compulsive traders, flitting in and out of the market, pretending to be able to outsmart the system. Less than one tenth of them hold their investments for less than one year. Most are in holdings which they *hold*. About one-third (32 percent) hold their investments for more than six years.

Almost universally, the wealthy are fairly unimpressed with the current trend to extol the virtues of high investment risk as though there were some automatic connection between risk and riches. Those who excel hold their principal in high respect—higher even than the rate of return. Consciously or not, they hold to the investment philosophy, "The return *of* your principal is more important than the return *on* your principal." When the sole focus comes down to bloating the rate of return, people lose sight of the value of the principal itself. Their greed glands take over and they are destined for disappointment. Proven wisdom from Adam Smith, author of *The Wealth of Nations*, is, "The first law of money is not to lose it." Those who attain genuine financial success today still heed those words despite the fact that they are two hundred years old.

Doesn't it stand to reason that if God wants to use mortal experience to teach eternal lessons and instill eternal qualities in his children, he would encourage us by other means than tactics built on greed, haste, and impatience?

GOAL-SETTERS IN ALL THINGS

Another key characteristic mentioned in the survey deserves notice. Financially successful people are zealots when it comes to goals. They use goals and goal-tracking fervently. In their businesses, in their occupations and careers, in their household management, and in their saving and investing they set goals. They use the goals to measure and analyze progress. President Thomas S. Monson stated: "When performance is measured, performance improves. When performance is measured and reported, the rate of improvement accelerates." (CR, October 1970, p. 107.)

Goal-setting gives the aspirants another huge advantage. They use long-term goals as a means of tempering their impulses, insuring steady, vigorous progress. Our passions are powerful forces for good when they are harnessed; they are the source of our undoing when they are not. In virtually any endeavor, people fail because they do not subordinate their impulses to their overall mission and higher purposes.

Nowhere does this hold more true than in the realm of money management. Although we seldom like to admit it, when you get down to a cellular level, a purchase can be a hormone-laden, passion-filled experience. This has actually been scientifically documented. Human beings have been hooked up to the EKG and EEG monitors and plopped down in front of a television tuned to QVC or the Home Shopping Network. When some tantalizing trinket or bauble is traipsed across the screen, scientists can verify the dramatic alterations in the very physiology of the viewers. Their pulse rates increase, their heart rates elevate, their respiration becomes more rapid. When they dial ten digits on a phone and recite sixteen digits on a piece of plastic they often have an emotional catharsis.

Apparently none of us is immune to such temptations. We must learn to override them, sticking to our plans and higher intentions. Back in my financial dark ages I can vividly remember attempting to convince Susan of what a smart financial move it would be for us to have a sports car as a family vehicle. One's mind can come up with some great lines of logic (or illogic) when really put to the task: "Susan, these little beauties are easy to park and maneuver. They get terrific gas mileage because they are so light. And boy, do they hold their value! Why, I know a guy that bought one of these fifteen years ago and. . . ." She didn't buy it (my rationale) and consequently neither did I (the car).

People with well-defined goals and a bit of commitment are powerful. They have more leverage in their moments of enticement and a higher likelihood of overcoming. Those who continually give in to their impulses and passions soon become enslaved by them. Remember the Law of Appetites, Passions, and Lusts: Spending money on appetites, passions, and lusts will intensify them rather than satisfy them. Ask any addict.

When it comes to money (and every other worthwhile pursuit), the real bottom line is *discipline*. Nothing else can serve as a substitute. Personal discipline is the rock upon which the wise build and over which the foolish stumble. Harry Emerson Fosdick said it well: "No life ever grows great until it is focused, dedicated, and disciplined."

BETWEEN THE LINES

The Lord does not squander time. Every moment of every one of our mortal days He instructs and helps His children to develop celestial traits and godlike characteristics. Many of those instructive lessons come through temporal systems like finances. You can be assured that as you develop the disciplined characteristics of the genuinely rich you are also developing the eternal attributes of the genuinely righteous.

God will use any and all righteous means to instruct His children. An unlimited being uses unlimited ways to fulfill His purposes. He employs types, shadows, symbols, metaphors, and meaning-fraught patterns to enlighten us and show us the way (see 2 Nephi 11:4; Hosea 12:10). The wise among us look for and see His ever-present messages in their everyday dealings, humbly amazed at the ubiquity of His teaching instruments.

FIVE

The Vision First

Clearly understood goals bring our lives into focus just as a magnifying glass focuses a beam of light into one burning point. Without goals our efforts may be scattered and un-productive. Without knowing it, we may be torn by conflicting impulses. (Ezra Taft Benson, *The Teachings of Ezra Taft Benson* [Salt Lake City: Bookcraft, 1988], p. 384.)

Among the ancient proverbs of Israel we find, "Where there is no vision, the people perish" (Proverbs 29:18). From that succinct expression comes volumes of insight. Vision constitutes the crucial element in the principle and power of what the prophets call faith. Everything in human endeavor comes from it. Everything we do stems from a vision in the mind of an achievement or an action that will produce a result which is as yet unseen by the physical eye. The eye of the mind sees it before the physical eye can behold it. Hear it from the Prophet Joseph Smith:

> Were this class to go back and reflect upon the history of their lives, from the period of their first recollection, and ask themselves what principle excited them to action, or what gave them energy and activity in all their lawful avocations, callings, and pursuits, what would be the answer? Would it not be that it was the assurance which they had of the existence of things which they had not seen as yet? Was it not the hope which you had, in consequence of your belief in the existence of unseen things, which stimulated you to action and exertion in order to obtain them? (*Lectures on Faith*, 1:11.)

For us to succeed in our financial endeavors we must develop a clear vision of what we seek. This must occur on several levels. We will begin in the same manner that we build a temple; we will begin with the foundation. Fundamentally, you must live and breathe one key philosophy. This core understanding can best be grasped by comparing and contrasting two words. The first is *acquirement*.

ACQUIREMENT MENTALITY

The dictionary defines *acquirement* as the act of obtaining, the getting or gaining by one's own efforts or action; and it's a perfectly good word. However, when it comes to money, an acquirement mentality on its own leaves much to be desired. The world teems with people huffing and puffing, plying their utmost skills in an attempt to acquire lots of money and material assets. But the acquirement of cash is not the real issue. It is not what you eat but what you digest that matters. It's not what you read but what you assimilate that counts. And this planet overflows with people who are prodigious acquirers but who will never know one day of financial peace.

Among too many financial gurus, the total focus centers on accelerating the acquirement. Everywhere you turn, someone is touting some new way for you to get your hands on more cash. The strategy hardly has to be recommended. Babylon is obsessed with acquirement. Throngs of people are feverishly ransacking the world, pushing relentlessly for *more*. "More what?" you may ask them. "Not sure," they respond. "I just know I need more something and probably a lot of it." They are driving themselves to early graves following a bad map.

A SUPERIOR WORD

Consider another word from the dictionary: *accumulation*. Accumulation is defined as the act of gathering and amassing. The distinction between accumulation and acquirement is crucial. People can acquire until they are blue in the face (and some of them do—where do you think the cartoonist got the idea of smurfs?) but it is those who are dead set on accumulation who actually get ahead.

Think of it. ACCUMULATION. Visualize yourself actually amassing a large pile of friendly, diligent, hard-working greenbacks. Try it. Picture yourself gathering and possessing a nice stack of crisp, clean money. If you are following my suggestion literally you are undoubtedly wearing a warm smile on your face. The image of stockpiling a Matterhorn of money is a fairly therapeutic thought in our stress-filled lives. And that is my point! Picture a vision of acquirement and you will sense your pulse rate rising and your breathing becoming labored. Acquirement connotes aggression, and aggression implies stress. The vision of accumulation on the other hand is peace-producing and reassuring.

As a foundation stone in your earthly temple, you want to build on accumulation. Time and time again, as I have interviewed people on the subject of money, I have seen a recurrent pattern—a pattern of salvation. Those who succeed do not put themselves on an acquirement treadmill. Instead they focus on retaining a specific percentage of their hard-earned dollars. They stock up and stash away a good, solid reserve of frisky dollars. They don't just acquire. They accumulate.

A CASE IN POINT

I know of a man who learned the hard way the decided difference between acquirement and accumulation. A physician by profession, he selected a growing community and, for a time, was the only practitioner in his specialty for miles around. He was a good doctor with good people skills, and within months his practice skyrocketed.

Within a few years, however, despite his earlier burgeoning practice and the kind of dollars he must have then been generating, he filed for bankruptcy. Here is the story as I heard it.

In getting through medical school he had accrued sizable debts that were followed by the costs and debts of setting up a practice with a new office building, furnishings, and equipment. As the practice took off, and with such great prospects ahead, he decided to plunge into the construction of a luxurious home—one that he felt would "fit the image" of a prospering physician.

Not long after this, with the demand for his services increasing and personal needs for cash mounting, he expanded into a larger, nicer facility, a new clinic with more space and, of course, more image. All this he was doing on borrowed funds with the help and emphatic encouragement of his bankers, accountants, and financial advisers. He had a great future, could write off the interest and could "shelter" some income. It all seemed so good, on paper. But in reality it brought more debt, which meant greater pressure on his practice to produce cash flow.

With the lion's share of his income going to debt service, he often felt cheated in his spendable dollars as he worried about meeting monthly obligations. Even though his practice remained healthy, he was "maxing out." Under the load, in time the harness began to chafe. With few discretionary dollars available, he financed expensive toys in an attempt to ease his lot.

After a while, growing impatient with the slow growth of spendable money, he ventured into some speculative investments he thought would get him "over the hump" and, at the same time, create some tax shelter. He borrowed money to do this, hoping to repay the loan out of the profits he planned to make. But in fact these investments failed to perform as expected, so rather than solving the problem they added to the burden. Some of his ventures went completely belly up. He lost money on every hand. By now the cash flow had drifted into the negative.

Worst of all, the pressure killed his love for his profession. With longer hours and more patients per hour, naturally, the quality of his work diminished. Sensing this, some of the patients found services elsewhere. This reduced his income, which increased the pressure. He had put himself into a tragic tailspin, spiraling downward, headed for the crash of bankruptcy.

Let it be written in every heart: Acquirement never was happiness. This man had to become a world-class acquirer to discover that. May each of us learn from his experience.

THE LAWS OF ACCUMULATION

Eternal principles are stunning in their simplicity. Though they exert profound effects upon the universe and upon our lives, they can often be expressed in such simple terms that small children can comprehend them. Prepare for the utmost in simple, comprehensible financial strategy. There are only two laws to master in order to *accumulate* money:

LAW NO. 1: DON'T SPEND ALL YOU EARN.
LAW NO. 2: DON'T LOSE WHAT YOU SAVE.

Accelerated acquirement is not the medicine, because insufficient *acquirement is not the disease.* Compared to most of our brothers and sisters in other parts of the world, we in the United States actually have little problem in acquiring money. It rolls through our fingers at mind-boggling rates. Too many of us simply do not live the two fundamental laws cited above, and we wind up allowing the money to go out the back door as fast as it comes in the front.

You do not have to be Marilyn Vos Savant or Albert Einstein to understand the laws of accumulation. Even young deacons can understand and apply these principles. You do not have to subscribe to savvy newsletters. You do not have to graduate from Harvard, be clairvoyant, be excessively talented, beautiful, or slim. What you have to do is picture yourself living these two laws and let that vision govern your actions thenceforth.

SIX

COMMITTING TO ACCUMULATION

If you wish to get rich, save what you get. A fool can earn money: but it takes a wise man to save and dispose of it to his own advantage. (Brigham Young, JD, 11:301.)

A significant number of Heavenly Father's children never get beyond "paycheck-to-paycheck living." They can describe their pain and frustration with the situation in great detail. I know this because during my seminars they tell me so. When I ask them, "Why are you living paycheck to paycheck?" I get several standard answers: "My employer isn't paying me what I'm worth," or "My boss won't give me a raise," or "Things cost too much these days," or "My spouse doesn't make as much as he [or she] should, " or "The government doesn't do enough." The list goes on, but I won't—you have the idea.

Not one of those answers gets to the real heart of the matter. When all the excuses and rationalizations are laid aside, people live paycheck to paycheck because they live paycheck to paycheck. Wait, before you sarcastically say to me, "Well, duh Deaton, that's brilliant." Hear me out. Spending one's entire paycheck is not due to demonic external forces; it is due to inner weakness. People who never have anything left never have anything left because they spend it all. There is no end to the irony of that. If you are frequently short of cash before the arrival of your next paycheck, you had better wake up. The problem is YOU!

People keep thinking it's about the size of the paycheck. It's not. "Paycheck-to-paycheck syndrome" is about discipline and commitment. Thousands of high-income earners still find themselves stuck in paycheck to paycheck living, because they never take control of their monetary life. Until they learn to govern themselves and commit themselves to live within their means they will never escape the syndrome.

THE SPANISH IMPOSITION

In the middle of October, people in the United States acknowledge the arrival of Christopher Columbus to the continents now called the Americas. Columbus claimed the land, which *they* called the Indies, for and in behalf of the Spanish monarchy. Over the ensuing decades the Spaniards ransacked these continents. They gathered up boatloads of gold and silver and turquoise and precious spices and shipped all those riches back to Spain. Yet history plainly records that the Spanish monarchy went bankrupt. Benjamin Franklin's chilling quip ought to sound a warning to us all: "The Indies did not make Spain rich, because her outgoes were greater than her incomes." (*The Autobiography and Other Writings, The Way to Wealth, 1758* [Bantam Books, 1982], p. 189.) You see, the gain in Spain went mainly down the drain. (Where are Audrey Hepburn and Julie Andrews anyway? You can never find a good soprano when you need one.)

Ultimately, the only accurate and valid answer to the question "Why do I live paycheck to paycheck?" is: "I have not made an all-out commitment to accumulation." Unless and until we make that inner change, nothing will ever substantially alter in our monetary life, no matter how much we make. In fact, without that inner control, more money will be more of a curse than a blessing. Our mistakes will just take on bigger proportions and sting a great deal more.

THE RICHEST MAN IN BABYLON

Let me share a story that will offer a tried and proven way to get out of paycheck-to-paycheck syndrome.

In 1926 George S. Clason, a financial writer for eastern newspapers, wrote a series of "Babylonian Parables" dealing with personal financial management. Later the articles were gathered and published as a book under the title of the best known of these short allegories. That book, *The Richest Man in Babylon*, has since become a financial classic. I strongly endorse its concepts and recommend you read it at least once a year and teach it to your offspring.

Here's the Cliff Notes version of the parable: Schooled by a wealthy elder, a young man named Arkad progresses from a hand-to-mouth existence to become the richest man in his country, Babylon. Arkad's biggest breakthrough comes when his mentor emphasizes that he must grasp that *a part of all he earns is his to keep*. At first Arkad does not get it. In rebuttal he declares that *all* he earns is his to keep. Patiently his teacher points out that he must pay others to make his way through life. A portion of his earnings of necessity goes to others in compensation for the goods and services he receives from them. But if *all* his earnings pass through his fingers, he will wind up as little more than a slave, working for his food and raiment.

Forcefully the wise elder impresses upon Arkad a grand key. He must learn to pay himself first, before he disburses a single penny from his earnings. Arkad learns to set part of his income aside so that it may be put to use earning as well. And that's what Arkad does. Living on 90 percent of his income, he soon finds that his lifestyle has not diminished very much but he has gained a great advantage. He now has some money to put to work so that *it can do some earning* as well, and the numbers of workers grow with each paycheck. Arkad soon gains the full vision of how powerful it can be to live within one's income. He has mastered the first steps in becoming a successful financial steward.

GETTING BEYOND PAYCHECK-TO-PAYCHECK LIVING

The lessons Arkad learned will pay huge dividends for you too. You must:

1. Live on less than you earn.
2. Pay yourself first.

These two rules cure paycheck-to-paycheck syndrome and they go together. The best way to live number one is to live number two. Pay yourself first! Every month. No matter what. Decide on a certain fixed percentage, and do it. Set your "extra" aside *before* you do anything else. Live on the remainder. That's the answer. If we expect the "extra" to show up *after* we are done spending, it will never happen. Granted, at first putting aside the "extra" is not easy. But once people make the commitment and practice it for a few months, it does become easier.

A major building block in the life of President Heber J. Grant was a quotation he read from Ralph Waldo Emerson that went something like this: "That which we persist in doing becomes easy; not that the nature of the thing has changed, but that our power to do has increased." This principle is an eternal one, and through the monthly exercise of the first two rules from *The Richest Man In Babylon* we develop spiritual muscle.

There is of course no magic potion, gadget, or software that we can buy to give ourselves commitment and discipline. That is a gift we have to give ourselves by exercising self-restraint. No one ever gets out of paycheck-to-paycheck syndrome until he or she makes the "No-Matter-What Commitment" and then puts that commitment into action.

ONE STEP HIGHER AND BETTER

George S. Clason could have called his idea the "Ten-Ninety Rule"—save and invest 10 percent of your income, live on the remaining 90 percent. Time has proven this concept to be extremely sound and valuable. People who have practiced the Ten-Ninety Rule have prospered substantially on an earthly level because they are living a law that improves the mastery of their spirit over their body. The Lord approves of that and rewards accordingly. Yet all Latter-day Saints should know that, as solid as it may be, the Ten-Ninety Rule is a lesser or preparatory law. We can do even better.

Brother Clason did not understand the law of tithing. (By now I trust he has been duly instructed and converted in the spirit world by our missionaries over there.) We must take his recommendation to a higher plane. Rather than living the Ten-Ninety Rule, we can take a superior road and live the Ten-Ten-Eighty Rule. We invoke and secure divine promises and blessings when we live the law of tithing and pay the Lord first (see Malachi 3:10-12). The Lord's servants have repeatedly and plainly declared it: Strive to the full extent of your own ability—keep the commandments, work diligently at your occupation, pay your tithes and offerings, and leave the rest up to the Lord. An example of following this counsel comes from President Joseph F. Smith:

> A short time ago I met a brother—I need not call his name, for he is but one among thousands who can bear the same testimony, not only by the word of mouth but by the evidences of thrift, of prosperity, of progress and of improvement which surround him in the midst of the deserts. This season he has gathered in rich harvests, his farms having produced in abundance, while the farms of many of his neighbors are clogged with weeds, and their harvests have been only one-half or one-third what his has been.
>
> How do you account for it? I account for it in the fact that God has blessed him; and so does he, for he is an intelligent man, a man that not only labors wisely and prudently, but in the fear of God, and in the desire of his heart to obey his laws. He said to me and my companion with whom we were traveling: "God has blessed me because I have striven to keep his laws, and because I have been true to my family." He went out there upon the desert seven or eight years ago, impoverished by persecution and exile, being driven from his home and from his affairs, compelled to wander in exile for years, part of the time preaching the gospel. He returned seven or eight years ago, and settled down upon the desert. Today, out of the earth, the burning sands, he has produced beautiful homes, he has fruitful fields, which are spread out before the eyes of any man who wishes to go and look upon them.
>
> He pays his tithing, he remembers his offerings, he is obedient to the laws of God, and he is not afraid to bear testimony to his friends and neighbors that it is through obedience that

God has blessed and prospered him, and made him what he is today. He is not the only one; there are others who are prospered in like manner. And I testify that it is because God has blessed him, and his soil, and his labors, that he obtained the increase, and secured the blessings for which he sought and labored. He has acted in good faith with the Lord: the Lord has known his heart, and has blessed him accordingly, and he is prosperous today in that desert, while as to many of his neighbors—go and look for yourselves at their broad acres. They tell the story for themselves.

His lands are clear from noxious weeds, because he has labored, and taken care of his lands, and because God has inspired him, and enlightened his mind. The Lord has blessed him in his basket and in his store, in his labors and in the thoughts of his mind, he has been inspired and enabled to accomplish the work that he has done: I testify that it is because of [this] man's faith in the promise of the Lord, and his desire to obey his laws, that he is blessed and prospered of him. (Joseph F. Smith, CR, October 1897, pp. 35–36.)

I love this example! How plain! How explicit! As you strive to do *all* that you can do, during that very process the Lord is able to pour out greater blessings because you are fulfilling your part of the law of grace. And by grace we are saved. This is the formula—the pattern of salvation—in every context. If you comprehend this one lesson, you have grasped the celestial interchange between faith, grace, and works, which most of Heavenly Father's children never quite figure out.

Trust in the Lord and His promises without restraint or compromise. Work hard and live the Ten-Ten-Eighty Rule. Pay Him first. Set aside the Lord's full 10 percent before you do one other thing. Then pay yourself a like amount, and then make all of your life and lifestyle decisions on the remaining 80 percent. Sometimes the math may not appear to work out. It doesn't have to. You are invoking higher laws than the math of accounting. You are triggering the incomparable law of grace in your behalf.

One final admonition is warranted. Pay a *full* tithe. Do as the Lord says. Put Him to the test!

> Bring ye all the tithes into the storehouse, that there may be meat in mine house, and prove me now herewith, saith the LORD of hosts, if I will not open you the windows of heaven, and pour you out a blessing, that there shall not be room enough to receive it.
>
> And I will rebuke the devourer for your sakes, and he shall not destroy the fruits of your ground; neither shall your vine cast her fruit before the time in the field, saith the LORD of hosts.
>
> And all nations shall call you blessed: for ye shall be a delightsome land, saith the LORD of hosts. (Malachi 3:10-12.)

Knowing the Lord's generosity and His promises made in this matter, one wonders why so many Saints do not seem to enjoy more of the blessings promised in the law of tithing. Could it be that many of them do not pay a *full* tithing—perhaps withholding something, or in some way rationalizing some compromise on what they pay, thus forfeiting the promised blessing?

I leave the introspection up to you. Are you living the law of tithing fully? Do you fulfill your part of the law of grace? Reflect upon it and pray about it. If you have the spiritual confirmation that you are living the level of law that the Lord expects of *you*, then continue forth and be not weary in well doing. If not, then you know what to do about it.

SEVEN

COMPOUNDING YOUR SUCCESS

Seeing every act of our lives, every decision we make, as patterned toward the development of a life that shall permit us to enter into the presence of the Lord, our Heavenly Father, to gain which is to obtain eternal life—how much more wisdom there would be in the many things of life. (Harold B. Lee, *Stand Ye in Holy Places* [Salt Lake City: Deseret Book, 1974], p. 102.)

The parable of the Richest Man in Babylon goes on to teach one other useful principle. To learn it we must return to the story.

Twelve months after the first lesson has been taught, the wealthy elder returns to check on his pupil. "What progress have you made since I last saw you?" he asks. "I have paid myself faithfully," Arkad replies, also explaining that he has put his money to work, earning interest. Algamish (the elder) commends his student and asks Arkad what he does with the interest. Arkad answers: "I do have a great feast with honey and fine wine and spiced cake. Also I have bought myself a scarlet tunic. And someday I shall buy myself a Corvette! (Ooops, sorry) . . . a young ass on which to ride." At which Algamish laughs and says, "You do eat the children of your savings."

Algamish, the elder teacher, goes on to explain a great principle of prosperity: Each gold piece Arkad earns and saves is a worker, who can not only work but can have offspring, who can not only work but can have offspring, who can not only work but can have offspring, who. . . . Summing up, Arkad's mentor states, "First get thee an *army* of golden workers, then many a rich banquet will you enjoy without regret!"

38

Rule number three from *The Richest Man in Babylon*:

3. Let your savings compound.

What you earn—your 10 percent—must earn and beget other earners as well. Thus we learn that the interest accrued on the 10 percent is not to be spent until you have reached your financial freedom goal. Those dollars remain in the fray, earning and begetting more earners month after month. This is the principle of compounding.

WHAT AUNT POLLY DOESN'T KNOW

One of the lovable characters from American folklore is Mark Twain's artful knave Tom Sawyer. Well known is the episode in which Tom has been assigned by his Aunt Polly to paint the fence, a task he does not relish. Indignant, he unenthusiastically begins the project of applying the paint by himself. Before long, however, Tom's keen mind develops a plan by which to extricate himself from the hands-on drudgery. He soon figures out a way of employing the labor of others by conveying the impression that whitewashing a fence is some sort of sport. Within minutes, several of Tom's friends are enjoying all the fun of completing Tom's task for him. Young Mr. Sawyer winds up completing the job in a hands-free supervisory role. (Mark Twain may be credited with having written the first American management text.)

Two lessons can be learned from Tom Sawyer's methods. First, what constitutes "work" and what constitutes "play" is a matter of perspective. One person's work is another person's recreation. The second lesson is more applicable to our current topic. There are basically two ways of getting a job done: do it yourself or employ the labor of others. When it comes to accruing a living income you can work for money, but you can also put money to work for you. Ultimately, if you live long enough, not even the first choice will be an option. Those who do not learn how to put money to work for them are all set to experience grim repercussions in their old age.

LET YOUR SAVINGS COMPOUND

Let the power of compounding work for you. Venita Van Caspel, an author and financial consultant who lives in Houston, Texas, stated, "In my opinion, the 'eighth wonder of the world' is not the Astrodome, but compound interest!" (*Money Dynamics for the 1980s* [Reston, Virginia: Reston Publishing Co., 1980], pp. 26–27.) Albert Einstein, who needs no introduction, was asked by a reporter to cite the most amazing mathematical formula he ever encountered. His answer was "Compound interest." To appreciate their high esteem for compounding you need to see the difference between simple interest and compound interest:

Simple Interest is interest paid only on the principal. The interest accrued is viewed as accumulating apart from the principal. No interest is paid on accumulated interest.

Compound Interest is interest paid on the principal *and* the accrued interest. At designated intervals (monthly, quarterly, annually) accrued interest is added to the principal, and during the next interval interest accrues on that new *sum*. At each interval, the total amount gaining interest increases. The interest of each interval is added and begins to gain interest thereafter, thus markedly enhancing the effective yield.

SIMPLE INTEREST VS. COMPOUND INTEREST

Figure 1 is an economic table that will illustrate the advantageous power of compounding. The initial amount of money invested is the same; in each case a lump sum of $10,000 is deposited. Both accounts receive 8 percent interest per annum. However, one account earns simple interest while the other has the interest compounded quarterly.

FIGURE 1

Yr.	Simple Interest			Compound Interest		
	Principal	Interest	Total	Principal	Interest	Total
1	$10,000	$200	$10,200	$10,000	$200	$10,200
	10,000	200	10,400	10,200	204	10,404
	10,000	200	10,600	10,404	208	10,612
	10,000	200	10,800	10,612	212	10,824
2	10,000	200	11,000	10,824	217	11,041
	10,000	200	11,200	11,041	221	11,262
	10,000	200	11,400	11,262	225	11,487
	10,000	200	11,600	11,487	230	11,717
3	10,000	200	11,800	11,717	234	11,951
	10,000	200	12,000	11,951	239	12,190
	10,000	200	12,200	12,190	244	12,434
	10,000	200	12,400	12,434	249	12,683
4	10,000	200	12,600	12,683	253	12,936
	10,000	200	12,800	12,936	259	13,195
	10,000	200	13,000	13,195	264	13,459
	10,000	200	13,200	13,459	269	13,728

As time passes, the difference becomes distinct and, eventually, quite noteworthy. After six subsequent years the table looks like figure 2.

FIGURE 2

Yr.	Simple Interest			Compound Interest		
	Principal	Interest	Total	Principal	Interest	Total
5	$10,000	$200	$14,000	$14,568	$291	$14,859
6	10,000	200	14,800	15,769	315	16,084
7	10,000	200	15,600	17,069	341	17,410
8	10,000	200	16,400	18,476	370	18,846
9	10,000	200	17,200	19,999	400	20,399
10	10,000	200	18,000	21,647	433	22,080

Over a ten-year period, while the annual interest rate is the same in both cases, compounding results in a net gain of $4,080—a greater return of over 22 percent.

THE RULE OF 72

There is a handy little rule that can help you make quick mental computations on the growth of your nest eggs. Called the Rule of 72, it is a simple way of determining the time required to double your principal. To determine the time it takes to double your money at any given interest rate, simply divide 72 by the interest rate. If, for example, you are earning 8 percent on your money, it will take nine years to double your money ($72 \div 8 = 9$). Applying the same formula, if you are earning 10 percent on your money it will take you a little over seven years (7.2) to double your present principal.

Peter Minuit Finagles Manhattan

Many of us have heard in a long-ago U.S. history class that a certain Peter Minuit of the Dutch West India Company made a shrewd land deal. In 1626 Minuit supposedly "purchased" the entire island of Manhattan for $24 worth of costume jewelry. (As it turned out, the native Americans who actually received the jewelry were not even in the tribe that held possession of the island. So you can decide for yourself who duped whom.)

"What a deal!" exclaimed the history teacher. At first glance it would seem so. The land Minuit obtained, the primest of prime "beach front property," now values in the tidy range of $25 to $40 billion. Land value has grown impressively, but another rationale is also quite instructive. Observe the growth of the Minuit family fortune (figure 3) if Peter had banked that $24 and the family had averaged a 6 percent return, compounded annually:

FIGURE 3

Year	Account Value
1626	$24
1726	$8,143
1826	$2,763,000
1926	$937,500,000
2000	$70,000,000,000
2026	$300,000,000,000

Rather than a $35-billion parcel of land, *which they would have had to maintain and manage,* the Minuits would have, currently, roughly twice that much. By the four hundredth anniversary of the "great land deal," in the year 2026, the Minuit bank account would stand at over $300 billion. Pretty impressive.

Here is another example of the power of compounding.

Lump Sum of $25,000 at 8 Percent

Suppose you achieve a savings account of $25,000 by age 30, and that you could average an annual interest rate of eight percent, compounded annually. Your lump would grow as per figure 4.

FIGURE 4

5 years	$ 36,733
10 years	$ 53,973
15 years	$ 79,304
20 years	$116,524
25 years	$171,212
30 years	$251,566
35 years	$369,634

Eight percent per year is a reasonable expectation for long-term investment horizons, like 35 years. Yet the pleasant surprise for all of us is that, through the miracle of compounding, we have actually done considerably better than that. What percentage growth in terms of simple interest did we actually achieve on our $25,000? Subtracting the original sum, we have a gain of roughly $344,000. That is an increase of 1,376 percent! Dividing that increase by 35 years, we discover a wonderful surprise. We have averaged 39.3 percent growth *each year*! The effect is very rewarding—when *you* are the lender. And if you pick the right vehicles (more on that later) you have low risk and few maintenance worries.

THE INFLATION FACTOR

At this juncture it might be good to start thinking about real spending power. We will take this into full consideration when we create the Wealth Plan, and you might as well get used to the idea. Along with the power of compounding you must also be aware of a counter force—inflation. The dollar you invest is going to decline in purchasing power with the passage of time. The creep of inflation subtracts value from your nest egg and underscores why we must invest wisely in order to surpass the effects of inflation.

If we step back in time and take an actual historical example, you will see what it all means. I choose a period in the history of the U.S. economy that includes both favorable and unfavorable inflationary episodes, the period from 1952 to 1987. Economists say that the dollar lost approximately 78 percent of its value during that 35-year period. Putting it another way, it took four and a half dollars in 1987 to buy what you could buy in 1952 with one dollar.

Let's put the inflation factor into our previous example and see if there was a gain or loss in *actual purchasing power*. After 35 years we have made $369,634 from our initial investment of $25,000. If we divide this by 4.5, we will put 1987 dollars back into the 1952 context:

$$\frac{\$369,634}{4.5} = \$82,141$$

In other words, $82,141 in 1952 would buy what $369,634 would buy in 1987. (If this shocks you a bit, relax—I will give you better news later on.) So in terms of the original frame of reference (1952) we *have* made a gain. Our $25,000 has grown to $82,141 in equivalent purchasing power. Despite the ravages of inflation, we have still forged ahead. Although it may not be as dramatic as you first thought, you are still ahead of the game. You have more than tripled your purchasing power.

By now you have undoubtedly noticed that the real power in compounding comes in the *latter* stages. Time is the biggest factor in the equation. The sooner you get to harnessing this power, the more dramatic its effects in your behalf.

Let me illustrate this point with figure 5:

FIGURE 5
$25,000 at 8 Percent, Compounded Annually

Time	Total Amount	Gain	% Gain	% Gain Per Year
5 years	$36,733	$11,733	47	9.4
10 years	$53,973	$28,973	116	11.6
15 years	$79,304	$54,304	217	14.5
20 years	$116,524	$91,524	366	18.3
25 years	$171,212	$146,212	585	23.4
30 years	$251,566	$226,566	906	30.2
35 years	$369,634	$344,634	1,379	39.4

The greatest benefits from compounding are accrued in the *long-term* context. As you let the money grow, each year adds to the value of each of the preceding years. In this last example, if the money works for twenty years, you gain 18.3 percent on your money *each year*. And if the money works an additional five years, the percent gained *for each year* increases to 23.4 percent!

A Dramatic Comparison

Take a look at what a dramatic difference two investors experience (figure 6). Both investors earn 10 percent on their money. Both save $2,000 per year. Investor A, however, starts early. She starts at age 25 and contributes $2,000 per year for eight years and then stops. How much did Investor A put in all together? $16,000.

Investor B procrastinates for those eight years and then gets going. Let's say she puts in her $2,000 each year for the succeeding 28 years. How much did Investor B invest in total? $56,000. Now notice the salient truth: Investor A fares better! Investor A winds up at age 60 with a total of $362,817, and Investor B has only $295,262! Moral of the story: Start early— start now!

FIGURE 6

	Investor A			Investor B	
Age	Tax-Deferred Contribution	Year-End Value	Age	Tax-Deferred Contribution	Year-End Value
25	$2,000	$2,200	25	$0	$0
26	$2,000	4,620	26	$0	0
27	$2,000	7,282	27	$0	0
28	$2,000	10,210	28	$0	0
29	$2,000	13,431	29	$0	0
30	$2,000	16,974	30	$0	0
31	$2,000	20,872	31	$0	0
32	$2,000	25,159	32	$0	0
33	$0	27,675	33	$2,000	2,200
34	$0	30,442	34	$2,000	4,620
35	$0	33,487	35	$2,000	7,282
36	$0	36,835	36	$2,000	10,210
37	$0	40,519	37	$2,000	13,431
•	•	•	•	•	•
•	•	•	•	•	•
56	$0	247,809	56	$2,000	194,694
57	$0	272,590	57	$2,000	216,364
58	$0	299,849	58	$2,000	240,200
59	$0	329,834	59	$2,000	266,240
60	$0	362,817	60	$2,000	295,262
Less Total Invested		(16,000)	**Less Total Invested**		(56,000)
Net Earnings		**$345,817**	**Net Earnings**		**$239,262**

ACCUMULATING A MILLION

Here is another way to visualize the miracle of compounding: What does it take to save *a million dollars*; that is, how much money would you have to put aside if your goal was to save one million dollars? The answer depends on how much you want the resource of time and the power of compounding to assist you.

Let me show you. Let us suppose that you could get an annual interest rate on your money of 9 percent compounded quarterly. Here is a sequence showing how much you would have to deposit monthly and how long it would take to achieve the goal. I am going to put this example in table form, but I am going to do so gradually in order to emphasize the power of compounding.

YEARS	TOTAL PAYMENTS	MONTHLY PAYMENT
5	60	$13,280

In other words, if you wanted to save $1 million in five years you would have to save over $13,250 per month for the sixty-month period. Now, that is a lot. Not many could do that out of their own earnings. So harness the power of consistency and a little patience and watch what happens. Continuing:

YEARS	TOTAL PAYMENTS	MONTHLY PAYMENT
10	120	$5,186
20	240	$1,510

By doubling the time frame, we make something interesting become evident: it reduces the amount you have to save by much more than half. Why? Because you are making earnings on the earnings. Your first generation of "workers" is begetting offspring who are now also working for you, and *both* generations continue to produce a larger *third* generation, which also works and begets. And so on; each generation becoming larger and more powerful. The process starts slowly, but it begins to "snowball," and with the passing of time the momentum builds.

To show you how reasonable the goal can be, here is the rest of the table:

YEARS	TOTAL PAYMENTS	MONTHLY PAYMENT
30	360	$554
40	480	$218

Another View of This Premise

There is another way of looking at this whole scenario that will also illustrate the power of compounding. I hope this will make a deep impression on your mind.

Using the selfsame parameters as described above, I want you to see how much of "your own money" is involved at the various plateaus. At the end of each of these scenarios you wind up owning $1 million. The amount you had to actually *earn* by the "sweat of your own brow" is what I want to highlight for you.

YEARS	MONTHLY AMOUNT	TOTAL AMOUNT YOU DEPOSIT
5	$13,280	$796,800

In this case, you have saved $1 million and you have received some benefit from the compounding of interest, but not much. The net message here is that you had to earn and deposit the vast majority of those dollars yourself. You had only about 20 percent of your goal contributed by interest.

If, however, you are willing to be patient, you can reduce your earning burden significantly. Continuing:

YEARS	MONTHLY AMOUNT	TOTAL AMOUNT YOU DEPOSIT
5	$13,280	$796,800
10	5,186	622,320
15	2,658	478,440
20	1,510	362,400
25	902	270,600
30	554	199,400
35	346	145,320
40	218	104,640
45	138	74,520

The power of compounding comes through loud and clear. In the case of the thirty-year program, your workers have accomplished over 80 percent of the work. The good news in all of this is that you can achieve the million-dollar mark without a lot of worry, distraction, or management on your part.

In summary, becoming a millionaire is within the reach of anyone who really *wants* it. Save $900 per month at 9 percent (compounded quarterly) for twenty-five years, for example, and you will achieve that notable goal.

THE ETERNAL LESSON

At least two lessons need to be learned. One: The longer you employ the power of compounding, the better you offset the effects of inflation. Two: Procrastination must be rooted out of your character. Monetarily and spiritually, procrastination stands as a dreaded enemy.

And now, as I said unto you before, as ye have had so many witnesses, therefore, I beseech of you that ye do not procrastinate the day of your repentance until the end; for after this day of life, which is given us to prepare for eternity, behold, if we do not improve our time while in this life, then cometh the night of darkness wherein there can be no labor performed (Alma 34:33).

Once again we can see what Father is teaching us. Procrastination is bad enough when it applies to our temporal context. How much more dramatic are its penalties when it applies to our eternal salvation! Not one excuse justifies delay. The sooner we get started the better. We cannot change the past, but we can seize the moment and make the very most of our future—temporally and spiritually.

EIGHT

Defining the Vision

I am decidedly in favor of practical religion—of everyday useful life. And if I today attend to what devolves upon me to do, and then do that which presents itself tomorrow, and so on, when eternity comes I will be prepared to enter on the things of eternity. But I would not be prepared for that sphere of action, unless I could manage the things that are now within my reach. You must all learn to do this. (Brigham Young, JD, 5:3–4.)

No one stumbles onto financial freedom. It is not obtained through luck or some quirky stroke of fate. Financial freedom is a strategically planned destination achieved only by those who seek it and apply the correct principles to achieve it. A strategic plan presupposes a strategic vision. That is where we begin. We are going to create a custom-tailored vision of a freedom reservoir.

THE RESERVOIR PRINCIPLE

In the western states we enjoy the benefits of an ingenious system of water repositories called reservoirs. When the hardy pioneers came to these arid lands they met conditions quite different from what they had known in the eastern river valleys. The territory was parched and the rainfall was sparse and unpredictable. (Except in Arizona. Here things are more predictable—we *never* have much rain.)

To sustain crops and livestock and make communities possible the early pioneers went up into the mountains and dammed off the streams and rivers, creating lovely man-made lakes. These reservoirs offered much to the valleys below, and they still do. They are places of beauty and recreation. Fish and wildlife flourish in and around them. They also provide security and peace of mind, for in the summer, when the rain is slight, the water stored in the reservoirs supplies our needs. Herein lies a great symbol. Monetary reservoirs offer the self-same benefits. We all need to create a monetary reservoir—a lake of liquid financial security.

The laws for creating reservoirs are simple: When outflow *equals* inflow you have "river." When outflow is *greater than* inflow you have "drought." When outflow is *less than* inflow you create "reservoir." The longer inflow exceeds outflow, the larger the reservoir becomes. And once the reservoir has been established, outflow can be equal to inflow and the reservoir will remain. The reservoir stays, and so do all of the attendant joys and benefits.

This metaphor also illustrates the difference between acquirement and accumulation. Those who focus primarily on acquirement confuse the rain with the reservoir. But to secure some peace of mind you must do more than make it rain hard once in a while. You must implement ways of *collecting* and *conserving* that rainfall. Picture having a brimming lake of liquid assets large enough to provide all the income you need for the lifestyle you desire. To see what such a reservoir would look like, in numerical terms, we need to answer three questions, A, B, and C:

A. How many years until your retirement?

Keep in mind that we are not working some hypothetical example here. This needs to be *your* life we are planning. If you plan to work up to the traditional retirement age of sixty-five, subtract your current age from sixty-five. If you plan to be actively earning up to some age other than sixty-five, use that age. If you are working this as a couple (and you should if you are married), choose the date when both of you will be done with active earning.

B. What will the rate of inflation be for the rest of your life?

Don't ask me; I don't know. (And you can quote me on that if you want.) If you don't know either, that puts us both in some respectable company. In the past, several very reputable research entities have made predictions about what inflation would do. Even when they focus only on the coming decade, their attempts fail. Too many factors play into the scenario. The task amounts to trying to predict the unpredictable. Nobody knows for sure what inflation will do over the course of a lifetime, so in a way I am asking you to put down your own wrong answer. (Honey, is our crystal ball still in the attic?)

Despite the fact that we cannot be absolutely certain what inflation will do, we must bring it into consideration. Inflation is real. Make no mistake about it. The impact of inflation is one of the single biggest factors in your financial future. Many of our grandparents, unaware of inflation (inflation was what they did to an inner tube), overlooked that factor as they planned for retirement. Most of them, having lived through the Depression, were more diligent than we in setting aside money for the future. Unfortunately, too many of them thought that a dollar would always be a dollar. And in a certain sense that was not the case.

A WORD ON INFLATION

A rose is a rose, but a dollar is not so constant. The dollar today does not buy what it did even one decade ago. For example, in the thirty years from 1956 to 1986 (again, a period in which we had both high and low inflationary episodes), overall the dollar lost 74 percent of its value. In other words, a dollar in 1956 would buy four times what it would in 1986. If the dollar *diminishes*, why do they call it *inflation*? The answer has to do with the law of supply and demand. The value of the dollar deflates whenever the number of dollars inflates disproportionately. When the government prints and puts into circulation more money than the rise in goods and services warrants, the value of the dollar falls. Inflated numbers means deflated value.

Inflation is not new. Inflation has been around for centuries, and that is not necessarily bad. Almost all economists agree that a mild amount of inflation is actually healthy. The core issue about inflation is the *rate* at which the inflation is occurring. In America during the 1950s and early 1960s inflation averaged about two percent per year. The dollar lost value, but the rate was low and the impact on purchasing power was gradual. In those days people paid little attention to inflation. In the 1970s inflation became a household word as it rose to six percent per year and increased to nearly nine percent in the latter half of that decade. The *rate* of inflation accelerated to the point where people could actually feel the effect.

At the outset of the 1980s, when inflation hit 19 percent a year, people awoke. The dollar was shrinking and they *knew* it. They could feel it at the grocery store, at the automobile dealership—everywhere. Clerks would come up and raise the price of an appliance right in front of you while you were thinking about buying it. And if you did decide to buy it, and did not sprint to the check-out stand, the price went up two times on your way to pay for it—or so it seemed.

This awakening had its good points. Most people realized they could not retire at today's values and had to give some forethought to future values. The ones who got caught in the vise were the souls who retired in the '40s and '50s. Many thought they had planned for an adequate monthly income. But by the end of the '70s they found themselves in an uncomfortable pinch. Their income was fixed, but their purchasing power was not. Every day they fell further and further behind. The government made some modest attempts to soften the pain with adjustments to the Social Security allotments. Despite those cost-of-living adjustments, though, many of our elderly wound up in near poverty. They were attempting to live on the number of dollars that once would have meant a comfortable income but today means destitution.

We have been forewarned. We know that inflation has not gone away and we had better darn well use that knowledge. You need to make some reasonable estimation of what inflation will do in the future, even if there is no way to be certain what that will be. Nothing is chiseled in stone anyway. You will have to make course adjustments along the way. I encourage you to run through this estimation procedure, which I am showing you in this chapter and the next, about every three years. That way, as you continue to monitor inflationary trends, you can make corrections as they are needed. To help make this decision less ambiguous, let me share three charts to show you what inflation has been in the past. Naturally, what inflation *has been* does not guarantee what it *will be*, but the information can be of some service as you make your estimation.

CHART 1
Inflation's History: 1950–1995
(Percentage figures are averages of 5-year intervals)

1950		1975	
	2.0%		8.1%
1955		1980	
	2.0%		7.5%
1960		1985	
	2.3%		3.6%
1965		1990	
	2.4%		3.6%
1970		1995	
	6.1%		

CHART 2
Inflation in the 1990s
(Source: U.S. Dept. of Commerce)

1990	5.4%
1991	4.2%
1992	3.0%
1993	3.0%
1994	2.6%
1995	2.8%
1996	3.3%
1997	1.8%

CHART 3
Historical Averages
(Source: U.S. Dept. of Commerce)

Average Annual Inflation Rate: 1926 –1997 = 3.1%
Average Annual Inflation Rate: 1950 –1997 = 4.3%

With this information make your choice. Do not use a fraction or a decimal. Choose a whole number.

C. In today's dollars, what annual income will you need for your retirement lifestyle?

Suppose for a moment that inflation just disappeared. Thinking in terms of what a dollar buys today, how much money would you need to cover your retirement lifestyle per year? Don't get in a hurry with this one. You need to consider several important questions. For example, where do you plan to live when you no longer generate active earnings? Cost of living, tax rates, and housing costs vary throughout the country. You can retire more cheaply in North Dakota than you can in southern California.

I encourage you to do a bit of research. Ask around. Talk to some people who are retired. In Arizona we have a wealth of retired people, whom we lovingly refer to as "snowbirds." From November to April they flock in from the northern tundras to clog our vehicular arteries, apparently forgetting that some of the rest of us want to get to work. In general, the snowbirds and the locals get along very well, except for the times when one of the snowbirds slams on the brakes in the middle of a wide-open intersection. You can see the driver, pointing for the benefit of all his passengers: "Oh look! There's another Safeway!" (I admit: My favorite Arizona bumper sticker is the one that says, "When I get old, I'm going to go *north* and drive slow.")

Seriously, a few polite conversations with a snowbird or two prove valuable. Most retired people are reluctant to tell you how much they have put away and what their sources are, but most of them are more than glad to honestly tell you what it costs to maintain their standard of living. It happens to be one of their favorite subjects, and your biggest challenge will not be to get them *into* the conversation but rather how to *get out* of the conversation when you want to leave.

Below is a partial list of considerations. You may want to include these questions in your interviews with your retired acquaintances. Above all, consider them carefully yourself.

1. Do you intend to own your residence (or residences) or rent it?
2. If you plan to own the home, will you have it paid for, or will you still be making mortgage payments? What will insurance cost?
3. How much traveling do you plan to do? Will you eat out a lot?
4. How many cars and recreational vehicles are you going to own?
5. How much will health care and medical insurance cost? (The answer to this question may blow your mind.)
6. How much will your income and property taxes be?

It is important to think of answer C as the *total* amount you need to live—your before-tax income needs.

Every person I have talked to who has conducted this survey has found it to be *very* enlightening and *very* useful. It opens their eyes to the realities retired people face. Explore the issue carefully. Try to look through the eyes of several people, so you get an accurate picture. Inquire of both single individuals and couples. Through your research you will be able to make a good decision, yielding a good figure for your calculations.

The most common rule of thumb used by professional retirement planners suggests that answer C should be approximately 70 percent of your current income. Let me hasten to add that the farther you are from retirement, the less useful this hint tends to be. For example, my daughter and son-in-law are just starting out in life. They have not even begun to reach their earning apex (at least I hope not), or the full magnitude of their lifestyle expenditures. For them to use this rule of thumb would be misleading. They are much better off using the method I previously described. If, on the other hand, you happen to be within five years or so of retirement you may find the rule useful.

An Example

Let me show you how enlightening all this information can be. The following exercise is meant to give you perspective, not heart failure. Before I bring the Boogie Man out of the closet (the one starring in the hit horror film, "The Innocents Meet Retirement Reality"), let me reassure you that the Wealth Plan in this book will bring you ample success.

Now for a brief appearance by the Boogie Man: Let us suppose you have come to the conclusion that your retirement income needs to be $40,000 a year in today's dollars. Let us further suppose that there will be no Social Security and no retirement or pension income from any source other than your own retirement savings. In other words, you are going to live solely off the interest derived from your savings. The formula to compute the amount of principal needed to sustain yourself is:

Annual Living Estimate

Rate of Return on Principal = Amount of Principal Required

Assume that you will make 8 percent per year on your savings. How big would your nest egg have to be in order to yield $40,000 per year? Plugging in the values, we get:

$$\frac{\$40,000}{8\%} = \$500,000$$

This means you would need to have $500,000, gaining 8 percent per year, to supply you with $40,000 to live on each year. Again, this is all in terms of today's dollars.

Now let's factor in time and inflation. As inflation creeps

along, eroding the value of the dollar, after a certain number of years a dollar will be worth one half of what it is today. This is called the "half-life of money." At an inflation rate of 5 percent, the half-life of money is just over fourteen years. This means that with inflation at five percent, money loses half its value every fourteen years. (Another way to see the scenario is to visualize prices doubling every fourteen years.)

Let us take as an example a twenty-three-year-old man who plans to retire at age sixty-five. His goal is to have, forty-two years down the road, the equivalent income of 40,000 of today's dollars per year (or about $3333 per month). If he fails to factor inflation into the picture, he will be destitute on $3333 per month when he gets to be sixty-five. Here is why: There are essentially three fourteen-year intervals between age twenty-three and age sixty-five. That means his purchasing power will be cut in half three times. Fourteen years from now, when the man is thirty-seven years old, $3333 will purchase only half of what it does today. In other words, he would have to get by on the equivalent of $1667.

The succeeding fourteen years amplify the damage. By the time the man reaches age fifty-one, his spending power will be cut in half once again. Essentially he would have to get by on the equivalent of $834. ($1667 ÷ 2 = $834.) In the final fourteen-year interval, just as he reaches retirement at age sixty-five, his purchasing power would be cut in half *once again*. The horror is straight out of a Stephen King novel. If our friend, forty-two years from now, had $500,000 in the bank, he would have to get by on what today is a paltry $417 a month. ($834 ÷ 2 = $417.) Now you see the grim reality inflation brings into one's retirement picture.

The horror doesn't end there. Inflation does not die the moment you retire. It keeps chugging right along, continuing its erosion *during* this man's retirement years as well. If he lives for thirty-five years after he retires, living to the ripe old age of a hundred, he would have to get by in the latter part of his life on the equivalent in today's dollars of $104 per month! All this despite the fact that he has $500,000 in the bank, which to us right now sounds like a fairly healthy sum.

Rushing to the point (so we can get on to the good news), in order to have, forty-two years from now, the standard of living that $40,000 per year would bring today, our friend would have to own a principal balance considerably larger than $500,000. The rude truth is he would need 8 times that much— a tidy $4 million. (Go ahead, faint.)

There is no question about it, Virginia; we have to plan ahead. At the same time we need not grow overly concerned at this point. Not all of inflation's effects are harmful. Although that amount of money sounds like a fortune, things are not nearly as grim as they might first appear. There are going to be strong favorable forces at work in your behalf, off-setting many of inflation's negative effects. Some of these forces will occur almost naturally. Others are going to be set in motion by your own efforts as you follow the Wealth Plan described later in this book.

DEFINING THE FUTURE

Now that you have answers for questions A, B, and C, we are ready to move forward. With the reality of inflation fresh in mind, we now add an inflation factor to your income estimate (answer C). We will call this estimate your **FI** (Future Income). As we proceed may I ask you to remain seated with your seat belt securely fastened around your waist. Keep your hands and feet inside the car, and have fun at all times. (I always wanted to work at Disneyland.)

Here's how to figure your FI: If your answer A is four or less, add 15 percent to answer C and use that sum as your FI. If your answer A is five or greater, then you will need to refer to the charts found in the back of the book in Appendix A. First locate the chart coinciding with your estimate of inflation (your answer B). If, for example, your estimate of inflation is 4 percent, use the chart on page 176. If your answer B is seven percent, use the chart on page 179.

After locating the appropriate chart, scan down the far left side of the table until you locate your answer A. Then move horizontally across the chart until you reach the column coinciding with your answer C. The number you find is your FI! (*Now*, panic.)

A Specific Example

Let me run an example so you can verify your own figures. Let us choose the following answers for questions A, B, and C:

A: Number of years to retirement 15
B: Inflation Rate 5%
C: Annual Income in Today's Dollars $50,000

First, since answer A is greater than five years, I refer to Appendix A. Because answer B is 5 percent, I turn to page 177. Moving down the far left side of the table, I find 15 (A) and then move to the right, horizontally across the chart, until I reach the column with the heading $50,000. The figure I find is $104,000. That's my FI. And here's what that figure means: Instead of planning for an annual income of $50,000, I need to plan for an annual income of $104,000. In other words, for my retirement dream to come true, I will need to expend *an average* of 104,000 of tomorrow's dollars per year in order to have the standard of living that someone has today at $50,000 per year.

Note that I emphasized *an average* of $104,000 per year. Assuming that retirement will last thirty-five years and that expenditures stay constant (and in most cases they don't—expenditures actually decline in the later retirement years because people travel less as they get into their nineties, and so on) my income need over that thirty-five-year period will *average* $104,000 per year. In the early years of my retirement I would not need that much. In my middle years of retirement, $104,000 would be what I'd need, and in the latter years, if the standard of living stays constant, I would spend more than $104,000 per year. But over the thirty-five-year period, the average annual income would be $104,000. In other words, our calculations have taken into due consideration the fact that inflation continues in retirement.

For many people, especially if they are in their teens, twenties and thirties, calculating their FI truly *is* what you call "Future Shock." Let me point out for your reassurance that your FI is in *tomorrow's* dollars, not today's. Once you see that, your FI figure will not seem so daunting. For one thing, the figure you are gazing at needs to be adjusted by the "Shirley Deaton Whole Milk Factor."

The Shirley Deaton Whole Milk Factor

(I'm glad you asked.) The Shirley Deaton Whole Milk Factor has to do with the "Relativity of Money." It is hard to believe right now, but thirty years into the future an annual income of $250,000 will seem as ordinary and commonplace as an annual income of $45,000 does today. Right now $250,000 seems like a very healthy income, but give it thirty years and your perspective will change.

Let me share a story. In the late 1950s, as a boy in my early teens, I was sitting in the back seat of an ugly, green station wagon. My parents, Jim and Shirley Deaton, were conversing in the front seat. My mother was doing an emotional "come-apart" because the dairy people had just done something dastardly. They had raised the price of whole milk from $1.00 per gallon clear up to $1.04 per gallon. Now, that doesn't seem like a big deal to you at this moment. That's because your mind-set about the price of milk is adjusted to present reality. The difference between $1.00 and $1.04 seems laughable. And that's part of my point. Back then, four cents bought something. Today it doesn't buy anything. To my parents this was a big price jump, and this was back in the days when milk came in a nice, sterile, glass bottle and the dairy people delivered it right to your doorstep.

Now picture this. Imagine me, Shirley's brilliant little son, piping up with something like this: "Mom, I have seen the future. Let me clue you in. In the future, Mom, the milk doesn't come in a glass bottle, and they won't deliver it to your doorstep either. You will have to go to the grocery store and get it yourself. It's always on the back wall of the store, and it won't come in a nice, sterile, glass bottle anymore. It will come in a plastic container (smeared with some unspeakable goo). In addition to the goo, Mom, there will be some weird black stripes on one side of the container. When you take the milk to the check-out stand the clerk will wave the container over a red light, and right before your eyes—like on a TV screen—there will flash up the message that this gallon of whole milk is going to cost $2.65!"

If my dear mother could have possibly believed this bizarre story, when she heard the price of whole milk at $2.65 per gallon her blood-curdling scream of agony would have shattered every window in the car. To her, you see, $2.65 would have been an outrage that signified the end of western civilization. She could not have imagined being able to feed a family at such outrageous prices. "$2.65 for milk, indeed! What is the world coming to?" (If you live in California, you are asking, "Where can you find milk that cheap?")

To complete the picture, you need to appreciate that my father was generating a good middle-class income in the late '50s, bringing in $9,000 a year. If, at that point in time, Jim and Shirley had done their calculations for retirement, the way you have, their FI would have been $45,000 to $50,000 per year. (They would have choked.) In the '50s, $50,000 was a movie star's income. Yet, guess what? That is precisely what happened. They now need $45,000 per year. Fortunately, because my parents lived the principles in the Wealth Plan, they have enough and to spare. Their freedom reservoir pumps out more than enough for them. They live comfortably. Mom has her refrigerator stocked with those goo-smeared plastic jugs of milk, and she doesn't bat an eye at the $2.65 she pays.

For my parents, the really good news is that they are not spending any of the principal in their freedom reservoir at this point. And, by the way, that is what we have calculated for you as well. Our wealth plan for you will also assume that you will not spend much, if any, of the principal you will have in your freedom reservoir. All that money you can leave to your children so they can have a big fight over it after you're gone, never speak to one another, or ever attend another family reunion. (Think of the money they'll save on phone bills alone.)

So don't be shocked or dismayed if your FI seems a bit out of reach at this point. There is plenty of good news to come as we unfold the Wealth Plan. Just be grateful you have been awakened. If you are gainfully employed, inflation is not as harmful as for those on fixed incomes. During your lifetime, inflation has been eating away at the dollar, yet you have been able, relatively speaking, to keep pace. It is when you *stop* working, and have to survive on a *fixed* income that inflation becomes so vicious. Being aware of that fact allows you to implement the measures to ensure happy days ahead, even after you have ceased to earn a monthly salary.

Before we go to the Wealth Plan, I would like to mention one more thing. Although we have equated having a freedom reservoir with retirement, to simplify description in this book, I am not implying that the whole point of life is to get to retirement as quickly as possible. Neither am I equating success in life with ample retirement, no matter how luxuriously it may be furbished. As Latter-day Saints we know that such a perspective is shallow and not what this book is about at all.

Financial freedom is not to be equated *solely* with a comfortable retirement. We have taken this focus, temporarily, in order to appreciate future values and the relativity of money. One cannot be financially free, in my opinion, without providing for one's future, but as important as that is, it should not be your sole purpose or your exclusive destination.

Aunt Agnes

Some experiences never fade from memory. One of my vivid recollections is of an occurrence that took place shortly after my wife and I were married. Like most young couples, we started with nothing. We both worked; and we rented a small apartment from a well-to-do woman, whom we affectionately called Aunt Agnes. One evening after work, as we sat chatting with our landlady, the subject of life's perspectives came up. Our wise friend took the opportunity to instruct two young pupils. Aunt Agnes told us of her marriage and the hopes and dreams she and her husband had held when they first married. They were diligent, she explained, and they set a goal to retire well. Agnes observed that, in essence, that was their *only* goal.

They committed themselves to the goal and worked hard. They earned good money through the years, selected a mutual fund, and made substantial monthly investments. As the U.S. economy grew and prospered, their dollars multiplied. By the time they had reached mid-life, they had a luxurious retirement in the offing. Then Agnes's husband died. In the prime of life, only a decade away from their golden years, he was gone.

Agnes lived in a comfortable home, drove a nice car, dressed well, and had not a financial care in the world. There was nothing wrong with that. She was grateful that she and her husband had planned and prepared for the future. She was much better off than most of her peers. Yet she had a monumental point to impress upon my young bride and me: "Don't spend all your money on the future. Enjoy some of it now."

We had heard the adage "Don't go barefoot all your life, so they can bury you in silk slippers," but Agnes instilled it in us. She explained, in retrospect, that she and her husband had gone too far in their focus on retirement. That being their *only* goal, they deferred *all* their enjoyment. She said they seldom took a trip, seldom went to dinner and a movie, seldom spent much of their money on each other. It went to the necessities, the children, and all the rest went into the retirement fund. Her words still echo, "There is more to life than preparing for retirement."

Agnes made a great impression on us that evening, one we have not forgotten. We slipped into our little apartment that night, clutching an important concept—the real wealth in life is life! We need to enjoy and be grateful for every day. One day is just as precious as another. A balance must be maintained. One must—absolutely must—prepare for the future, but must *live* in the present. Delayed gratification is a hallmark of mature and successful people, but even that virtue can be taken too far. Tomorrow should not take total precedence over today. A wholesome balance must be struck.

Obviously, just as touching and often more tragic are the examples of the converse. Too many people reach retirement age woefully unprepared for the future. People who fiddle all their time and money away in their youth, like the grasshopper in the ancient fable of "The Grasshopper and the Ant," wind up in grinding poverty and even degradation in their advanced years. In the final analysis, financial freedom has a lot to do with the direction in which you are moving and a *balanced* way of traveling. (And that perspective holds true regarding your journey back to the Father's presence as well.)

NINE

Defining the Freedom Reservoir

We must do more to get our people prepared for the difficult days we face in the future. Our major concern should be their spiritual preparation so they will respond with faith and not fear. "If ye are prepared, ye shall not fear" (D&C 38:30). Our next concern should be for their temporal preparation. (Ezra Taft Benson, *The Teachings of Ezra Taft Benson*, p. 264.)

Perspectives in place, it is time to really define your destination and how far along the path you have already come. You have learned what time and inflation do to future purchasing power. You are about to learn some good news about what time and interest will do to overcome that.

Now that you know your FI, what annual income you'll need in order to have your freedom lifestyle, the next questions are, "How much will I have to have in my freedom reservoir to generate my FI every year?" and "Where will that money come from?" One thing is certain—we had better not plan on Social Security supplying our entire reservoir. Those people today who are totally dependent on Social Security are clearly on the low end of the economic scale. Many are impoverished. Even those who receive the maximum benefits allowed under the system and no other income are barely above the officially defined poverty level.

As a point of reference, let's look at the sources retired people draw upon to fund their lifestyles and what the income percentages look like today. Currently, in the United States, successfully retired people fit the following profile:

Retirement Income Profile

Social Security. 25%
Personal Savings 25%
Employer's Retirement Plans 50%

In interviewing a reasonable sample of retired people, one finds that the successful ones derive about one-fourth of their income from Social Security (most of whom are getting the maximum benefits). They derive another quarter of their income from personal assets, like mutual funds, CDs and rental properties. The remaining half usually comes from some type of qualified retirement plan sponsored by the company they worked for or the business they created themselves. Such qualified plans offer several advantages and comprise a good share of the income sources for retired people today. Further up the scale, those who are in a stronger financial position are even less dependent on Social Security. They are virtually self-sufficient and live almost entirely on their dividend and interest income, coupled with money from their qualified plans.

The foregoing is a simplified statistical profile, presented for orientation purposes only. You definitely want to consider the same sources, but you need to adapt the percentages to your personal situation. If you are doubtful about Social Security's future you are not alone. A recent Harris poll reported that more Americans believe in the actuality of UFOs than believe in the viability of the Social Security Fund. However, things may not be nearly that bleak. *Kiplinger Personal Finance Magazine* recently reported: "A recent Gallop poll showed that 53% of Americans age 35 to 54 expect no benefits from Social Security. But in fact today's forty-something generation can count on bigger checks—after accounting for inflation —than 1990 retirees receive."

Clearly there are decisions and judgments to be made. I suggest caution about how much you depend on Social Security, especially if you are three decades or more from retirement age. Even for the so-called "Baby Boomer Generation," counting on the government for as much as 25 percent of future income may be a bit naive and risky. Only you can make that call for yourself.

Take this advice: Verify the current status of your own Social Security account. This is easy to do. Call: **1-800-772-1213**. Ask for **Form SSA-7004,** the *Request for Earnings and Benefit Estimate Statement*. You may be pleasantly surprised about how promptly it will arrive—five working days in most cases. The form is a cinch to fill out. It won't take more than about ten minutes. (You can also fill out your form via the Internet if you like; www.ssa.gov will get you there.) Within five to seven days you will have a statement of your account back in the mail. Not only can you verify your projected benefits, but you may also discover errors in your account. This can be good news, because it's much easier to make the correction before you start receiving benefits than after. Starting in 1999 you won't even have to order the form. The government will send you a statement at the end of each year, updating you on your account and benefit status.

A bit of good news: Social Security benefits are cost-of-living indexed, meaning that the amount you receive will substantially keep pace with inflation. If the government keeps its promise and continues that policy, you have one thing less to worry about. (I can see that didn't comfort you much.)

When your benefit estimate arrives you can subtract that amount from your FI to get what we will call your AFI (Adjusted Future Income). If you do not want to wait until your statement arrives, you can proceed to define your reservoir today.

STEP ONE: Decide what portion (percentage) of your FI you expect from Social Security:

_____ %.

STEP TWO: Adjust your FI accordingly:

If the decision is to count on Social Security for 20 percent of your income, multiply your FI by 20% and subtract that amount from FI to obtain your **AFI** (*Adjusted Future Income*).

Example

$104,000 (FI) X 20% (SS%) = $20,800 (Social Security Adjustment)

$104,000 (FI) minus $20,800 (SSA) = $83,200 (AFI)
ADJUSTED FUTURE INCOME

Remember that your spouse too may be entitled to some Social Security benefits. If so, be sure to include those benefits at this time as well. Subtract all combined benefits for you and your spouse from your FI in order to arrive at your AFI.

CHECKING THE RESERVOIR

Now we can really get down to business. Using a pencil, fill in the following form:

1. Enter Your AFI   _____

   FI after the Social Security benefit has been subtracted (see above)

2. Enter Any Pension Income   _____

Combine *all* sources of *annual* pension-type income. If, for example, you worked for the military for a while, and have a pension of $3,000 per month, enter $36,000. Many corporations pay part of their profits to their employees in the form of an annuity. If you and/or your spouse will have income from that type of source enter that in your total for line 2 as well. Also include income from any annuities you have dedicated to retirement funding.

Note: Most pension annuities are not cost-of-living indexed. If your pension income is indexed you should subtract that amount from your AFI before this step. Deduct it from your AFI first and then enter that amount in line 1, instead of line 2.

3. Remaining Future Income Needed   _____
    Subtract line 2 from line 1

Now we come to the big question: How much money will we need in our reservoir to produce that figure each year?

Here's how to figure the answer: As in a previous example, the rule of thumb is to assume 8 percent growth on your money during retirement. To find the lump sum needed to generate your needed income (line 3) divide line 3 by 8 percent or .08. Enter the answer on line 4.

4. Total Reservoir Needed At Retirement _____
    Divide line 3 by 8 percent (or .08)

Again, take a deep breath. If you have been doing some saving for retirement, you have some good news coming now. The next step is to list exactly what is set aside for retirement at this very moment. We will convert this figure into its future value. Then you can really see where you stand today in terms of the money you'll need tomorrow. Start by listing your current savings:

5. List and Total Current Savings
    a) IRAs/Keoghs/SEP IRAs   _____
       Present value of any and all IRAs, etc.
    b) Employer Retirement Plans   _____
       Present value of any and all 401[k], 403[b], or other sums in qualified plans. These are usually expressed as a lump sum on your annual retirement plan statements.
    c) Personal Savings   _____
       Present value of stocks, bonds, CDs, mutual funds, money market funds, etc.)

6. TOTAL AMOUNT SAVED   _____
    (Add all lines 5a -5c above)

Now that you have totaled your current savings, you are ready to project your principal into future terms.

7. Find Your Computational Factor   _____
    Refer to Appendix B, page 181

By multiplying your current savings by your computational factor you will see what compound interest will do for the money you have already saved.

8. Future Value of Savings   _____
    Multiply line 6 by line 7

To see how much more you need to save, subtract the future value of your current savings from your future income needed.

9. Current Savings Shortfall   _____
    Subtract line 8 from line 4

There it is, the truth! If line 8 is greater than line 4, you have done well. You already have sufficient assets working for you to meet your needs. Congratulations! If your line 8 is less than line 4, we will take one more step. We will now determine what you will have to save from this point forward to meet your goal.

10. Annual Savings Needed
    Refer to Appendix C, page 183   _____
                                      Yearly Savings Goal

Let me make one thing clear. This number is the *total amount* you need to save per year to reach your goal. You can now break this down into a monthly figure. If you are currently saving $500 per month and your computations show that you need to be saving $600 per month, this means you need to increase your monthly contribution by $100, not $600. The yearly savings goal is not how much *more* you have to save. This is the *total*.

There you have it. You have defined your financial future and determined where you stand. For some of you this may be terrific news and very reassuring. I hope that is the case. If it is not, at least you have been jolted into reality. And that is good news too. You can now swing into action and improve your situation.

In the Wealth Plan we will cover many useful ideas and methods for enhancing whatever situation you may be in. I have plenty of things to brighten your outlook.

THE WEALTH PLAN
You do not find until you seek

Two indispensable qualities characterize successful men and women: vision and discipline. They see what they need to do; and then they do it. The previous chapters supplied you with the vision of what to do. You must now move from the map to the journey. The Wealth Plan teaches you how to get on the road to financial freedom, from wherever you are now, and stay there.

TEN

THE WEALTH PLAN

PLANK NO. 1:
OWN A COVENANT-KEEPING MIND-SET

The Latter-day Saints are a covenant people. From the day of baptism through the spiritual milestones of our lives, we make promises with God and He makes promises with us. He always keeps His promises offered through His authorized servants, but it is the crucial test of our lives to see if we will make and keep our covenants with Him. (Henry B. Eyring, *Ensign*, November 1996, p. 30.)

Faith precedes the miracle, and covenant-keeping manifests and exercises faith. The Prophet Joseph Smith declared: "And as faith is the moving cause of all action in temporal concerns, so it is in spiritual. . . . As we receive by faith all temporal blessings that we do receive, so we in like manner receive by faith all spiritual blessings that we do receive. But faith is *not only* the principle of action, *but of power also*, in all intelligent beings, whether in heaven or on earth." (*Lectures on Faith*, 1:12-13; emphasis added.)

As well indoctrinated as we are in the power of keeping covenants—for the Apostles and prophets are fervent in their proclamations of it—most of us still don't get it. We are merely lukewarm when we should be on fire.

High achievers are strong-minded. They develop stalwart states of mind—something way beyond positive attitude. We are talking about a state of mind, called faith, brought on by

74

impeccable covenant-keeping, which can literally move the elements. To climb to those lofty pinnacles of power we must upgrade our respect for the whole process of giving our word and honoring it. In ancient cultures, swearing an oath—making a promise—giving one's word was as powerful as a written contract. Nephi recorded: "And he [Zoram] promised that he would go down into the wilderness unto our father. Yea, and he also made an oath unto us that he would tarry with us from that time forth. . . . And it came to pass that when Zoram had made an oath unto us, our fears did cease concerning him." (1 Nephi 4:35, 37.)

To instruct us in higher ways, Father in Heaven demonstrates at every turn in temporal life that the difference between mediocrity and power comes down to covenant-keeping. In virtually any pursuit of life, including money, those who succeed do so because they make firm commitments and then hold to those promises as if their lives depend on it. (Spiritually, that is literally the case.) That's where you must begin. The first plank in the Wealth Plan is to own a covenant-keeping mind-set. We are talking about an unshakable tenacity—something that will not wilt when pain occurs or pressure mounts—to live the Ten-Ten-Eighty Rule and bring your freedom reservoir into reality.

NOT HYPE BUT SUBSTANCE: NOT WISHES BUT COMMITMENT

Not long ago I had an appointment with a gentleman whose reputation for achievement in his field is virtually legendary. I wanted to meet him because several people, accomplished and respected in their own right, had said that he was a genuine example of a self-disciplined person. When I arrived at his office he was just concluding a meeting with one of his assistants. As the young man departed, I was invited to sit down. My host looked across the desk, and the first words out of his mouth went like this: "If people would just quit whining, grab their problems by the throat and attack them, they could make ten times the progress!" That is not a typical introduction. I knew instantly that it was going to be a stimulating interview. (And I wasn't disappointed.)

Explaining what precipitated the comment, my host briefly described how his assistant had made a commitment, but things had not gone as expected. Now he was rationalizing and looking for ways to renegotiate the commitment. My new friend went on to say, "If he would just let the commitment stand—quit trying to wriggle out of it, and just go to work—he would succeed. What is more, he would be stronger and better for it."

As we exchanged ideas and experiences I was strongly impressed with the forceful mind-set of this man. It was not just what he said, it was how he said it. There was an authenticity in his personal integrity that I have not often seen. Now that you have an idea of this man's character, let me add that he is extremely well-to-do financially. He is rich by almost anyone's standards. I hold that there is a direct link—a cause-and-effect relationship—between his character and his monetary success.

SOMETHING MONUMENTAL

"People have to learn to keep promises and commitments," he said. He continued: "I don't dare *not* keep my promises—whether to myself or another person. There is no difference, really. Every lapse weakens your character, and makes it that much harder to conquer the next rationalization. Before you know it, you have rationalized yourself into mediocrity, or worse." I was impressed with how seriously he viewed even "small promises." He seemed to be an anachronism, the last vestige of an out-moded era.

There was a time when a person's word was a binding contract. Back then people did not make promises, contracts, or commitments lightly—they thought about them carefully. Once made, those pacts were in force until the covenant was fulfilled. Contracts were not made to be broken for gain, or expediency, or simply for convenience, as is so often the case today. Technical loopholes, through which one might squirm, were totally beside the point. They were personally untenable—even reprehensible or repugnant. Karl G. Maeser taught it beautifully. "Place me behind prison walls ever so high, ever so thick, ever so strong, yet in some way, at some time, I may escape; but draw a chalk line around me and have me give my word of honor not to cross it, can I ever escape? No never! I die first!" (In Emerson West, *Vital Quotations* [Salt Lake City: Bookcraft, 1968], p. 167.)

This interview gave me much to think about. I decided that strong moral fiber is *not* the relic of some bygone era. It has been and ever will be the pathway to genuine success and riches. Although not widely practiced today, it still stands as the common trait in every truly great man and woman. Keeping everyday promises is something meaningful, even crucial. Few habits build character and personal power faster than keeping *every* promise. There is not only power in commitment, there is power *from* commitment.

There is something very definite that takes place inside you every time you keep a promise. It strengthens you. It adds power. You expand your capacity to accomplish bigger and better things. Each promise kept adds, and each failure subtracts. It is a simple and proportionate equation. The greater and more difficult the commitment, the greater the degree of empowerment when it is fulfilled. Keeping great promises brings great rewards, but no promise is too small or insignificant that keeping it won't add to one's personal reservoirs of strength.

In the final analysis the determinant in life's battles is not complex: strong people win; weak people lose. It is just that simple. And in practical terms one's strength is a function of how well one keeps covenants and promises.

MONEY IS A METER

Money can be a valuable tool in the process of learning to keep promises. To me, that is one of the greatest things money can do for a person. In a certain sense, money is the measurement system on the road to self-mastery. It can help you gauge, day by day, your progress in acquiring personal power.

My grandmother could translate many complex issues into simple terms. When I was a boy, she taught me: "You have mastered yourself when you can hear something bad about another person, and not spread it; when you can receive injury or insult, and not return it; when you can have money in your pocket, and not spend it."

The hardest of the three may well be the last. I am thoroughly convinced that one's ability to control money is a clear barometer of one's level of self-discipline. For many it is nigh to the ultimate test. Even in the Church many people can control every appetite and passion, can comply with lofty standards of conduct in every other aspect of life, but are totally out of control when it comes to the matter of money. Grandmother went on to say, "You can tell a lot about a person's character by how they earn their money, and how they use it."

When it comes to money, there is no substitute for discipline. And when rightly viewed, the converse is also true: When it comes to discipline there is no substitute for money. The two go hand in hand. If you want to become a strong, competent human being, master correct monetary principles. If you want to obtain and retain large sums of money, master correct self-management principles. You can look at it either way; building one builds the other.

MIND MASTERY

There is a simple reason why the first plank in the Wealth Plan focuses on mind-set. None of the other planks will work until you have firmly made up your mind to apply them. Giving in to oneself at the slightest twinge of pain is the hallmark of the mediocre. The powerful concepts in the remainder of this book will bring you freedom, but only when you put them to work. A firm commitment to do so must become one of your dominant thoughts.

Thoughts are the precursors of every action and every achievement. When we exert control of our minds, discipline our dominant thoughts, behavior and achievement take care of themselves. Behavior is mind driving body in fulfillment of dominant thought. The scriptures speak of the law of the harvest—"As you sow, so shall you reap." Nowhere does that law hold more true than in the garden of the human mind. Our thoughts are the seeds of our deeds. Whatever we do, we do first in the mind.

Here is one way to cultivate productive mind-sets. You can use it in many ways, and one of them is with money. Create "Strategic Signposts." It is not good enough to know that your savings and reservoir goals are here in this book or written in a notebook somewhere. You have to see them—think about them—several times each day. To keep your objectives out where you can be re-*minded* of them, take a few 3-by-5 cards and list these three essential ideas:

1.   ACCUMULATION, NOT JUST ACQUIREMENT.

2.   THERE ARE ONLY TWO LAWS OF ACCUMULATION:

    1.   Don't Spend All I Earn.

    2.   Don't Lose What I Save.

3.   A PART OF ALL I EARN IS MINE TO KEEP

    1.   Pay The Lord First.

    2.   Pay Myself Next—At Least Ten Percent Each Month.

    3.   Let My Savings Compound.

Underline the parts that will reinforce the concepts most emphatically to your mind. Place these signs in strategic locations, so that as you go through the day your thoughts will return to your commitment and reinforce it. Post one of your signs on the mirror where you shave or apply your makeup, one on the dashboard of your car, one on the door of the refrigerator, one on your desk, one on the inside cover of your organizer or planner, and, maybe most important, one on the cover of your checkbook. The consistent repetition will pay large dividends and will open the door to the rest of the Wealth Plan.

One more suggestion: Don't just read the signs. Think! The signpost technique works well, but you have to keep breathing fresh air into it or it will become stale and ineffective. After a few weeks the signposts may become familiar and commonplace. Change the cards once in a while. Put them in different places on the mirror—the upper left corner, instead of the right, for example. Change the color of the card or the style of the writing. Just taking the time to replace and reposition the signposts every two or three weeks will reinforce the commitments. As you rewrite or retype new cards you will be reinstating the concepts. Make the map a dominant thought, and major improvements will result.

A second way to strengthen commitment and build mindset is "Verbal Affirmations." This technique is especially effective for couples. Both partners must be totally committed to the objectives. The mind-set must be jointly shared. In some relationships this is a major obstacle. The partners do not communicate well and the issue of money separates them even further. The following technique helps overcome that. It fosters communication and reinforces each partner's resolve.

I know from personal experience that this technique works. Until this objective became a firmly entrenched mind-set for Susan and me, we held simple "commitment sessions." We would look one another in the eye, and hold a "one-minute pep rally." I would start. "A part of all we earn is ours to keep," I would say to her. In turn, she would say, "A part of all we earn *is* ours to keep." I would respond with, "Yes, a part of all we earn is *ours* to keep! We will not spend all we earn. We will not lose what we save." And she would reaffirm: "Yes! We are going to *accumulate*, not just acquire!" Maybe it was corny, but it worked.

We all go through moments of weakness. Mutual commitment strengthens you in those moments. We found it especially important to do this on Monday mornings. Getting back into the harness of the work week we reminded ourselves *why* we were going our separate ways. It was not just to acquire and spend. Breaking even was not good enough anymore. We reminded ourselves that we were going to win this week—to gain some ground on our financial dreams. In effect, we were promising each other that at the end of each month we would own more money than we did at the beginning of the month.

From small means were great things accomplished. We got tough. We worked on our weaknesses. Gradually, we got stronger. Our spending stayed in check. Our savings began, for the first time, to grow—really grow—not just bob up and down, as we put a little in and, a short while later, drew it out again. We learned to achieve consistency.

If you are single, this technique can still work for you—just get a mirror. Look yourself directly in the eye and affirm the commitments. Say them out loud. Repeat them and get into it. Affirm the concepts with conviction and certitude. Make up your mind, once and for all, that you are going to get mentally tough, stop pampering yourself, and become strong and financially free.

TWO HEADS, ONE PURSE

An unexpected and very significant by-product comes into a marriage because of the verbal affirmation technique. The key word in the rally is the word "our." Money can be the issue that either divides a couple or strengthens the relationship. Often the spouse who is doing the earning implies that money is more "mine" than "ours." (After all, whose name is on the paycheck anyway?) In subtle ways a spirit of division creeps in. Even in two-check relationships the feeling of "mine" and "yours" frequently exists. Abolish that type of thinking.

When the earner implies, "This is the money that I earned; be careful how you spend it," a destructive seed begins to germinate. Here and there the earner conveys resentment over expenditures by the other. The spender resents being resented. Soon the money becomes a wedge that divides the two. When the message, "I cannot trust *you* with *my* money," starts seeping into a marriage, the bell has begun to toll.

The daily "pep rally" effectively reverses that tide. It reaffirms that yours is a partnership. The money is *ours*. Who actually earns it is not an issue. You live together. You sustain one another in myriad ways beyond matters of money. You are a team. Neither could accomplish as much without the love and support of the other. By melding all of your resources, tangible and intangible, you are going to go farther and higher than either could go alone.

THE GREAT POWER OF SMALL MEANS

Sometimes just simple thoughts and modest methods produce enormous differences. The prophets have taught us two wonderful truths:

1. GREAT THINGS SPRING FROM SMALL BEGINNINGS.
2. BY SIMPLE MEANS ARE GREAT THINGS ACCOM-
   PLISHED.

From the invisible factory of a correct mind-set and firm commitment you will produce wealth and financial freedom. You, too, can do what others have done. The vast majority of the millionaires mentioned in the survey began with little or nothing. They did not get rich overnight in one wondrous act. They employed modest means and became money-wise and very rich.

ELEVEN

The Wealth Plan

Plank No. 2:
Own a Freedom Reservoir

This country has been named Deseret—the honey bee; and we all well understand the character of this little insect. It usually gathers more than it consumes, and lays aside a little. So should it be with the bees of the hive of Deseret. If we only earn fifty cents a day, we should try our utmost to live upon forty-five, and lay five cents away for "the rainy day." That is true economy, and was the counsel of President Brigham Young from my early recollection till the day he passed away. It has also been the counsel of his successors, and of all the leading members of this Church. (Joseph F. Smith, Collected Discourses, vol. 3, [Burbank, Calif.: B. H. S. Publishing, 1989], October 8, 1893, p. 401.)

If I could pass on only one sentence of financial advice to my children it would be "own a savings plan." That habit paves the way for so much, temporally and spiritually. Learn to discipline yourself to live on less than you earn. Pay yourself a fixed amount every month no matter what. It should not be less than 10 percent per month, no matter how little or how much you make.

Essentially there are two kinds of savings. The first category is the freedom reservoir, where the money saved and the interest earned should be considered unspendable until you have reached your "retirement" or "freedom" goal. The second type of savings occurs within your budget (the 80 percent part of the Ten-Ten-Eighty habit). Use this budgetary savings to prepare for large purchases or to reach short- to mid-range goals. The money and interest earned on this kind of savings is spent when you reach that particular goal. For now we will focus on the first category, the freedom reservoir.

SIMPLE SAVINGS

A good friend of mine has, over the years, ventured into numerous fields of "investment." He has owned stocks and bonds. He has put money into treasury bills and had a fling with gold, silver, and diamonds. He has been a limited partner in a couple of small business ventures. He has also invested in his share of real estate—his pride and joy being a lovely ranch in Wyoming, complete with livestock. In short, he has had his finger in just about every mainstream investment pie in America.

To this friend with broad investment experience, I posed the question, "What is the best investment you have ever made?" He thought about it for a few minutes, then responded: "You know, it's interesting. About six or seven years ago my wife and I decided to set aside five hundred dollars a month and put it into savings. We have found we can get along fairly well without that money. It doesn't seem to alter our lifestyle much. Every month we just put five hundred dollars in a passbook savings account until we accumulate $5,000. Then we roll it into a CD [Certificate of Deposit]. We have kept that going with a fair amount of consistency." He summed up with this key remark, "You know, to be totally honest with you, we have done better with that simple program than any investment we have ever made."

His next statement was also very meaningful: "By the time you figure everything into most of my investments—the commissions coming and going, the expenses, the legal fees, the accountants' fees, the taxes, and so on—I've never made any *real* money in any of those other things. Most of the time, I've actually lost a little. I'm really not what you would call a successful investor."

He was being open and honest, and I appreciated his candor. He may not be a successful investor, but he *is* a *typical* one. The truth is, most investors do not make all that much money when all is said and done, despite what they will say at the neighborhood parties. Later in this book we will develop a sound strategy for investing, and we will not leave our long-term investment money in CDs. Yet do not overlook my friend's message, spoken after years of experience. There is power in simplicity. Master a savings plan! Own it!

WHERE THE MONEY SHOULD GO

Now you have the Ten-Ten-Eighty Rule mastered, living on 80 percent of your income with 10 percent flowing into your freedom reservoir. The logical questions then become "Where should the reservoir money be placed? What vehicles should be utilized to maximize the results?"

First, if you have not done so already, create a modest emergency fund. Part of your reservoir should be liquid and accessible, held in something like a Money Market mutual fund. (I'll go into detail later.) I recommend the equivalent of three months' living expenses. If it takes you about $3,500 per month to keep your household going, you should have ready access to about $10,000 in case of an emergency (and I don't mean a white sale at Mervyn's).

TAXED VS. TAX-DEFERRED

The rest of the money, over and above the emergency fund, needs to be put to work in vehicles which offer you protection from the annoying pest we call income tax. The tax code allows for certain plans, commonly called "tax-deferred vehicles," to grow without yearly taxation. Taxes are postponed until the time of withdrawal, usually at retirement, between ages 59-1/2 and 70-1/2.

You cannot evade the tax man forever, but you usually come out way ahead if you can defer your settlement. In the accompanying chart you can see why. Assuming we are making 12 percent on our money and we fall into a 33 percent tax bracket, let us compare a tax-deferred account with one where the taxes are paid as we go along. If we put $100,000 in an account that gets taxed every year we wind up thirty years later with one million dollars. Taxes are paid and we can spend that million any way we want. Sounds good, right?

Look at the alternative. If we put $100,000 in a tax-deferred vehicle, we can postpone our settlement with the IRS until we reach retirement age. At that point, thirty years into the future, we wind up with 3.2 million dollars, but we still owe our taxes. Being in a 33 percent tax bracket, we wind up paying one million dollars in taxes and have a little over two million dollars for ourselves. We came out much, much better by deferring our taxes. Even if our tax bracket in thirty years goes to 50 percent, the tax-deferred account still fares better. We would still have $600,000 more by taking the tax-deferred route.

Taxed vs. Tax-deferred

Interest = 12%   Income Tax Bracket = 33%

	TODAY	6 YEARS	12 YEARS	18 YEARS	24 YEARS	30 YEARS
TAXED	100,000	159,000	252,000	400,000	634,000	1.0 Million
TAX DEFERRED	100,000	200,000	400,000	800,000	1.6 Mil	3.2 Million

I think I know your next question. "What are some good tax-deferred vehicles?" Well, there are three to consider.

1. Qualified Retirement Plans at Work

Far and away the best way to go, you can put *pre-tax* money into a qualified salary savings plan at work, like a 401(k), or a 403(b). Certain limitations apply. You can save up to 15 percent of your pre-tax income annually as long as the contribution does not exceed a certain limit. (In 1998 the annual limit is $10,000, but it is adjusted upward every so often and you should check on the current limit to be sure.)

In a qualified plan at work, you generally have several options as to where exactly your money may be invested.

Usually there is a menu of different funds from which to choose. In chapter 16 you will gain some insights that will help you choose the right types of funds for your investment horizon. Ordinarily these funds are products of the large fund families, like Fidelity, Vanguard, Invesco, to name just a few of the hundreds. Your money is pooled with money from other investors and thereby carries the name "Mutual Fund." Usually a mutual fund has a fund manager, who makes an annual commission from you and the other investors for making a bunch of shrewd moves to maximize your return. In the 1990s virtually every fund manager looked like a genius because we had such a robust bull market during that time.

What makes this option so attractive is that you can make money on some of the dollars that would have gone to Washington by way of taxes if you hadn't put them in your 401(k). Here's what I mean. Let's say you are in a 33 percent tax bracket and you have $1,200 per month that you do not need in your household budget. If you take advantage of your qualified plan at work, you can take the full amount—$1,200—and invest it. You get to defer your tax payment on that $1,200, along with all the growth you make on that money, until you reach retirement age. By contrast, if you use one of the other vehicles, you ordinarily have to pay the taxes on your income first and then you are allowed to invest the remainder. In this case you would have to reduce your investment principal by $400 and send that to Uncle Sam, which would leave you $800 to invest. *Big* difference.

2. Individual Retirement Accounts (IRAs)

Another option is to open an Individual Retirement Account (IRA). Depending on your income and whether or not you have a qualified plan at work, some or all of your contribution to an IRA can be deducted from your income tax. It comes right off the AGI—the adjusted gross income—on your tax form. The regulations are full of "ifs and buts," so check with your tax advisor or accountant to see if you qualify. Even if it turns out that you cannot take the contribution off your income

tax, an IRA can still be a good idea. Deductible or not, an IRA
offers you a way of putting money to work that can grow tax-
deferred. There are limitations here too: $2,000 per year per
individual, and $4,000 per year per couple.

An Individual Retirement Account is not an investment per
se. It is merely a provision in the tax law that allows you to
invest money without suffering a reduction due to taxes every
year. Once the money has been put into an IRA you must
decide how and where to invest it. The money can be put into
stocks, bonds, mutual funds, certificates of deposit, T-bills, and
a host of other vehicles. If you open a self-directed IRA you
have the freedom and the responsibility to invest the money
any way you choose (within some fairly broad limits, which
the government has spelled out).

3. Tax-deferred Annuities

One other option for tax-deferred treatment is an insur-
ance-related vehicle known as a tax-deferred annuity. The
money is invested with an insurance company. If you decide to
go this route, stick with one of the big name "blue-chip" companies. Avoid small companies that you have never heard of
(like Shifty of Scottsdale). Annuities are only as strong as the
company you are dealing with.

When you put money into an annuity you are ordinarily
granted a modest death benefit. If you should die before you
reach retirement, your beneficiary gets the death benefit or the
value of your investment, whichever is greater. The insurance
company offers you several choices in how to invest the money.
While the growth is occurring, no taxes are due. At maturity
you may either elect to "annuitize" (meaning you take your
money out gradually) or you may take all the money in one
lump sum. There are many options with advantages and disadvantages to each route. Your situation will dictate which is the
better choice for you, and a good insurance agent can educate
you on your options.

There are two types of annuities to consider, Single Premium and Flexible Premium. Single Premium means you do

not "make payments." It is a one-time shot. You simply take a chunk of money (the minimum is usually $10,000), open the annuity, and put the money into investment vehicles within the annuity. Flexible Premium means you start with an initial amount and add to it monthly, quarterly, or annually, as you go along. Your investment options within the annuity are the same as with a single-premium version.

THE PRINCIPLE OF CYCLES

Virtually every living thing grows through systematic patterns called cycles. These recurring sequences take the organism from one stage of development to another. The perennial cycle of plants repeats itself, rhythmically year after year, adding to or subtracting from the growth of previous years. Each annual cycle (micro-cycle) is a subset of yet another broader cycle—the overall life cycle (macro-cycle) of the organism itself.

The pattern of cycles is everywhere, a governing force in all living things. Mankind is not exempt. However, there is one difference in the cyclical growth of human beings. Much of the growth in our stages of development is discretionary. There is a fair degree of agency associated with our cyclical trends. We make the choices, choosing whether our cycles ascend or descend. Our life becomes the product of the micro-cycles we create.

We intuitively sense this truth. Near the end of each year we become contemplative and introspective. We evaluate our lives and progress. We mull and assess. Comparing one year's accomplishments to another, we discern trends of progression or retrogression. Vigorous growth occurs when we make sure the current micro-cycle exceeds the one before, knowing it is not just this one increment that is at stake but the expanded potential for even greater growth in the micro-cycle to come.

Combining the Power

The principle of cycles focuses our attention on a time-vindicated truth: We are in competition with no one but ourselves. The competition is to see if we can make each annual cycle as

effectual and significant as possible. In combination with other principles, these forces can be momentous. For example, we can combine
  1. Annual cycles
  2. Internal competition, and
  3. The power of simple means.

19____	SAVINGS JOURNAL		19 ____

ACCOUNT REGISTER

INSTITUTION	TYPE (CD, Passbook, etc.)	INTEREST RATE	PRINCIPAL	MATURITY DATE	VALUE AT MATURITY OR AT YEAR END

THREE-YEAR SUMMARY

YEAR	TOTAL DEPOSITED	TOTAL WITHDRAWN	NET AMOUNT	NET INCREASE/DECREASE
3 Years Ago: 19 ____				
2 Years Ago: 19 ____				
Last Year: 19 ____				
TOTAL				

MONTHLY JOURNAL

LINE		JAN	FEB	MAR	APR	MAY	JUN
1	Total saved monthly - previous year						
2	Projected monthly goal - current year						
3	Projected increase over previous year (Line 1-2)						
4	Actual monthly savings - current year						
5	Actual increase over previous year						
LINE		JUL	AUG	SEP	OCT	NOV	DEC
1	Total saved monthly - previous year						
2	Projected monthly goal - current year						
3	Projected increase over previous year (Line 1-2)						
4	Actual monthly savings - current year						
5	Actual increase over previous year						

ANNUAL SUMMARY

Projected Annual Savings (Total Line 2) ▶		Actual Annual Savings (Total Line 4) ▶	
		Total Life's Savings at start of current year ▶	
		TOTAL SAVINGS - YEAR END ▶	

Copyright© 1991, TimeMaxx   4555

A Method of Acceleration

If you would like to thrust the filling of your freedom reservoir into high gear, try this:

1. *Keep a savings journal.* Keep a record of your savings activity. This provides a fulcrum upon which self-disciplinary leverage can be applied. The accompanying form is an example of a good savings journal. The Monthly Journal section is particularly important. (See opposite page.)

2. *Record your monthly savings for one year.* In a previous chapter you determined your yearly savings goal. For the next twelve months record your performance in reaching that goal on a month-by-month basis.

3. *Determine to surpass yourself each year.* Compete with yourself. Make a commitment to surpass your previous record for the corresponding month. The idea is to make each month be a new record, topping the previous year's all-time high.

IMAGINE THE VICTORIES

Pause for a moment and reflect on the internal power this technique harnesses. Visualize yourself, having stretched to a new record, then unconditionally requiring yourself to shatter *that* record in the succeeding cycle. Never allow yourself to rest on "good enough." Accept only "better than ever before." Just think what that will do for your reservoir of money. Then think of what that will do to your reservoir of personal strength. This process, if turned into a perpetual habit, will vault you to absolutely stunning levels of progress. My grandfather told me, "The best compensation for doing something hard is that it increases your ability to do something harder."

I hope you will try this idea. Look for other ways to apply it. You will feel an excitement about doing better than ever before. The full value of this little technique will not hit home until you have actually applied it for sixteen to eighteen months. It takes twelve months to complete the first savings cycle. Once you have established your first baseline, the spirit of internal competition and the power of keeping every promise can work together. Throughout the second cycle you will have something to shoot for and something to surpass. You will find yourself saving like never before. You will be able to resist temptation and rationalization. The momentum builds, month after month and year after year, and so does your inner strength. By the third year the transformation in your self-mastery will be nothing short of phenomenal. The technique works, and it's potent. It derives power from the triad cited earlier—the power of cycles, the power of internal competition, and the power of small means—and it boosts your ability to keep covenants.

Do you see the huge spiritual implications of all this? Some people never learn how to properly channel their inner drives and powers. They spend all their time dissipating their energy, trying to surpass their neighbor. They would make infinitely greater progress if they would *internalize the energy* and work at surpassing their own records, year after year.

OFFER A REWARD

One more hint: Create a reward system to go along with your savings plan. At certain points, like milestones along a highway, prefix a series of rewards. For example, when you hit your savings goal three months in a row, agree to reward yourself with a weekend getaway or dinner at your favorite restaurant. Rewards add an element of fun and incentive to your quest. At each progressive milestone make each goal a little loftier and each reward a little bigger—enough to induce genuine incentive. Like rungs on a ladder, your rewards will inspire you to press forward, avoid splurging, and stay true to your mind-set of accumulation.

One clarification: Do not take money from your reservoir to fund the reward. Instead, work the rewards into your budget. Never consider your savings, or the earnings on your savings, as spendable until you have achieved the overall freedom goal.

In summary:

CHALLENGE yourself.
MEASURE yourself.
SURPASS yourself.
REWARD yourself.

I challenge you to harness the power of this lofty form of competition—the competition with self. It will prove to be the most potent expression of the competitive drives within you. The benefits you will derive are everlasting.

TWELVE

THE WEALTH PLAN

PLANK NO. 3:
OWN A TIGHT SHIP

It is to our advantage to take good care of the blessings God bestows upon us; if we pursue the opposite course, we cut off the power and glory God designs we should inherit. (Brigham Young, JD, 9:171).

Small leaks can sink great ships. Monetarily speaking, it is a wonder there are any ships floating at all these days. The use of readily available credit is so widespread that it has become a way of life for most people. Apparently they never stop to assess the leakage and the incredible damage occurring because of these very subtle ruptures.

Credit Card Buying

Let us suppose that Herb has a credit card with a modest $3,000 limit and has been carrying a balance of about $2,000 for quite some time. He has been making a few charges and making his regular token payments, keeping the balance fairly constant at $2,000. Lately, however, Herb has been tempted to buy some piece of electronic equipment that runs about $1,000. He reasons that he will hardly notice the increased amount added to his credit card payment. He is paying that anyway, and a few more dollars will hardly be noticed. So he does it. He makes his purchase and runs his card up to the $3,000 limit. Simple. Painless. Got what he wanted.

What will it take for Herb to bring things back to where they were before the purchase? If each month he makes the minimum payment required by his credit card—two percent of the remaining balance—and the APR (annual percentage rate) on his credit card is 18 percent (and many credit cards exact more than that), how much money will Herb have to pay to return his balance to the "original" $2,000? And how many months will it take? Take a guess.

The answers: Herb will pay the credit card company $3,770 and it will take him 79 months! Plus, he will still owe the $2,000! Financing one's purchases by credit card amounts to psychotic levels of generosity. Can you imagine Herb walking up to the check-out counter with this electronic trinket in his shopping cart and saying to the clerk: "You know, I see the sticker says $999.99, but I just don't feel right about paying you that amount. I'd really prefer to pay you three and a half times that much. How does $3,770 sound?" ("Security . . . Security to the front desk, please!")

Credit cards are great for convenience when placing orders, making flight and hotel reservations, and things of that kind. But they are *no way of financing purchases*. Using them that way is just dumb.

THE HIGH PRICE OF INSTALLMENT BUYING

Congress has enacted "truth-in-lending" laws that require disclosure of the costs involved in an installment purchase, but even that does not seem to wake people up. They keep blasting holes in their ships like there is no tomorrow. And the truth is: The truth-in-lending form tells *only part* of the truth! Here is what I mean:

Now what I am about to say has to do with installment buying. It is not about cars. I could have used living room furniture, computer equipment—any number of fun items as my example. I am just using cars as the example because of the universal experience.

Suppose a young man, age twenty-five, with $2,000 in the bank and a two-year-old car that is paid for, goes shopping for

a new car. He is thinking about something a little "classier"—
something with a little more "image." He finds an automobile,
with fine Corinthian leather, and falls in love with it. After driving his hardest bargain with the dealer, they settle on a price
of $20,000 for the new car. The dealer offers him a trade-in of
$5000 on the old car, gladly receives the young man's $2,000
from his savings, and offers him "easy credit terms" on the
remaining $13,000.

At closing, the dealer and the young man sit down to go
over the truth-in-lending form. Financing $13,000 at 10 percent
for five years, the payments come to $275 per month. The young
man is elated! He can make those payments and he is ready to
sign the contract, hardly caring what the fine print says.

According to the "TRUTH IN LENDING FORM," here's
the detail:

Principal. $13,000
Interest Rate: 10%
Number of Payments: 60
Monthly Payment:. $275
Total Payback (60 X $275). $16,500
Less Principal Financed. . . . . − $13,000
Total Finance Charge $3,500

TOTAL COST OF CAR . . . . . . ($20,000 + $3,500) = $23,500

By now the hormones are in overdrive and he gleefully
signs on the dotted line. He drives away with a shiny new car
and a coupon book, thinking that the total cost of the car is
$23,500 (assuming no late fees, of course).

Truth-In-Lending is really a misnomer; the figures only tell
the *obvious* costs. Let's look a little deeper into the matter. Suppose a young woman, also age 25, with $2,000 in the bank and
a two-year-old car that is paid for, goes shopping for a new car.
After thinking it over, however, she decides to stay with her
two-year-old car and leave her $2,000 in the bank. Suppose also
that she has the same job, the same lifestyle, and the same
expenses as the young man. They even live in the same apart-

ment complex and pay the same amount in rent and utilities. In summary, their income and expenses are pretty much identical.

The young woman learns from the young man that he went ahead and bought the car and is making payments of $275 per month. She reasons thus: "If he can get by without the $275 per month, so can I." But instead of *paying* interest with her $275, she adds it month by month to her original $2,000 nest egg and *receives* interest on her money.

At the end of the first year, what is the essential difference in their two lifestyles? Not much. They both lived without $275 in their monthly budgets. After the first year, he has a one-year-old car and twelve receipts, and she has a three-year-old car and a small bank account. Five years down the road, both are thirty years old, he has a five-year-old car and sixty receipts, and she has a seven-year-old car and a fairly nice bank account. (At that point everything on both cars will make noise but the horn.) If we assume the young woman made eight percent on her money, she would have approximately $23,000 in her account.

Suppose now she goes shopping for a new car. Car prices have gone up. After dickering with the car dealer she winds up thinking seriously about a car that costs $22,000. The dealer takes her old car for a spin and grants her $1,000 trade-in value, leaving a difference of $21,000. Then he asks her how much of that she wants to finance. She says: "Nada. I'll just pay cash." She takes $21,000 out of her purse and drives away in a new car with no payments to make and a measly little $2,000 left over, still sitting in the bank.

Now she reasons, "If the young man can live for the rest of his life without the $2,000 that I have in my bank account, so can I." How does she know he can live without the $2,000? Because he doesn't even know that it exists! He has been so busy paying interest with his money that he has not even seen that you can make money on your money by being paid interest. So she takes her paltry little sum of $2,000 and drops it into an index fund. (Yep, you guessed it. I'll describe index funds later.) She just lets that money compound for the next thirty-five years. At retirement, neither the man nor the woman can even remember the cars they were driving in their twenties and thirties, but she remembers her lowly little index fund. So she checks on what her account looks like now and she about faints. Her lowly little index fund has grown to an impressive $111,500! (That number is based on recent averages for index fund performance, 12 percent.)

What did that new car cost the young man at age twenty-five? It cost him $135,000! It cost him the obvious $23,500 and it also cost him the opportunity to make some money on his own money, which in the long run amounted to quite a sum. That is what most of us are not seeing. It's not just what's leaking in the form of interest and finance charges, it is what that money could be if it weren't leaking and it stayed with us to make money on its own. Will Rogers said it better than anybody else: "Interest! Them's that understands it, gets it. Them's that don't, pays it!"

Statesman John Randolph said: "I have discovered the philosopher's stone, that turns everything into gold. It is, 'Pay as you go.'" Too many people chase their lifestyle with their income, instead of providing their lifestyle out of their income. Thinking like "I'll soon be getting a raise," or "I'll be working a lot of overtime in the next few months," or "We'll be getting a tax refund next April"—such thinking gets us into trouble. We think we can spend what's coming instead of what we actually have in our possession.

The Value of Earned Money vs. Borrowed Money

People spend borrowed money less carefully than they do earned money. Borrowed money is hard to value. It does not seem all that much harder or more strenuous to borrow $14,000 than it does to borrow $12,000. People tend to spend more for a car—they do less shopping around, they do less bartering, they are less discriminating about options and extras, they are not as persistent in getting the salesperson down to the bottom line—when they finance a large part of it rather than paying cash for it.

I learned this from personal experience. One of the first cars I purchased was kind of a splurge. I paid dearly for it, too. I decided to finance a large part of it, and rationalized. I made only a half-hearted attempt to hammer on the salesperson and do some bargaining. (It was a pathetic attempt, really.) I wound up getting about every extra there was. The difference in the payments did not seem all that great. So I bought my car.

I enjoyed the car, and eventually I did get it paid for. During the period of my installments I came to realize the concepts I am sharing with you; and I grew wiser. A while later, I had accumulated $35,000 with one of those prestigious sports sedans in mind. The day I went shopping for the car the passions were percolating. The test drive proved the car was everything I had been dreaming about. Then the negotiations started, and I began to realize the power of this truth: *People are not as careful with borrowed money as they are with earned money.*

I had worked hard to earn the $35,000. And I had worked almost as hard to save it. That $35,000 chunk felt good in the bank, and the more I thought about taking that whole amount and exchanging it for a car, the more I examined the whole transaction in my mind. I began to weigh things more carefully. Reason started to deal with the passions.

I began thinking "I'm still going to get that car, but I'm not going to pay one cent more than I have to. Perhaps I can get the car and still have some of my cash left over." So I bartered and negotiated. I was so proud of myself; I wasn't my usual patsy self. After a couple of negotiation sessions the dealer caved in. Shopping around, checking the guides, talking to friends in the business, and playing one dealer against the other, I finally got the car down to a great price. And I still couldn't quite bring myself to do it. You would have thought the salesperson was going to drop dead when I said, "I'm going to think about it for another twenty-four hours."

On the way home I made my decision. When the passion had cooled and I was more rational about it, I could see there were better uses for that $35,000. I ended up driving a hard bargain on a car a step down from the first one. I gave up $20,000, kept $15,000, and felt 200 percent better about the whole situation. I was infinitely more thoughtful and frugal with money that I had earned and saved. It had value that was *real*. It was a whole different story from when I borrowed most of the money for my car.

It all comes down to stewardship. Part of being a good steward rests on getting the best value for every dollar you earn. Paying interest is poor value, and so is paying more than you need to for an item. When you are spending the dollars you have saved, your perspective is sharper. You sense the real value of your money, make better judgments, and stop many leaks in the hull of your ship.

THE FORTUNE HIDDEN IN YOUR HOME MORTGAGE

A substantial savings in interest can be accrued by accelerating the payment of *principal*. This works for any loan. Prepaying principal on large, long-term loans, like a mortgage on a home, can amount to the saving of a small fortune. You give up something in deductions on your income tax form, but you will more than make up for it in peace of mind.

Let's say, for example, you have a thirty-year, $150,000 mortgage at 8.5 percent. The monthly payment is roughly $1,150. By increasing the monthly payment slightly, just $150 per month, making the payment a nice round $1,300, you will accrue a savings of over $100,000! The extra $150 goes directly to the principal, reducing the balance faster. In this case a full ten years would be lopped off. The loan would be paid off in twenty years instead of thirty.

30 years (360 payments) @ $1,150 = $414,000

20 years (240 payments) @ $1,300 = <u>$312,000</u>

$102,000

At the end of the 20 years, your loan would be paid. If you then make *yourself* the payments ($1,300 per month) for the next ten years you will add a tidy little sum to your reservoir. At 8 percent compounded quarterly, you would have a bonus of over $237,000!

"YOU'LL NEVER SEE SAVINGS LIKE THESE AGAIN"

Seems like it should be simple. Saving is saving. Spending is spending. This is not exactly quantum physics, I know, yet somehow we lose track of the simple truth amid a mass of advertising confusion. The line goes like this: "You can save a bundle right now if you will come right down and spend some money."

If you sit in front of a television for any length of time you will be exposed to that ploy a dozen times. Advertisers have stricken the word *spend* from the dictionary (Quick, Emma, call *Unsolved Mysteries*), banishing it to advertising's outer darkness. Tell me you haven't heard something like this before:

> Ladies and gentlemen, boys and girls, come to our Fourth-of-July, year-end, close-out, going-out-of-business, inventory liquidation, first anniversary, over-stocked, everything-must-go, SALE-A-THON! You have never seen SAVINGS like this before! Everything in the entire warehouse [I was hoping he would say planet] has been marked down! Way, way down! SAVE like never before! With prices like these you cannot AFFORD to wait another minute! Get down here right away! You may never see SAVINGS like these again! Everything has got to go! The SAVINGS are going through the roof! If you're like me (and I know *I* am), you won't want to pass up a chance to SAVE THIS MUCH! Pack up the kids, pack up the granny, pack the car, and pack up your troubles in your old kit bag and get down here while the savings last!! This is a once-in-a-lifetime SAVINGS extravaganza! (Did I mention there would be free hot dogs, and balloons for the babies?)

As I write this, I cannot keep from smiling. What I've written is not *that* far off the real thing. I was trying to overplay it a little bit for the sake of humor. I couldn't do it. It was as over-hyped as a person can make it. It is already bloated to the hilt. (The only thing that slowed me down was that I ran out of exclamation points on my keyboard.)

The hucksters use every word in the book, except that you

will *never* hear the word spend. It is always *save*. Why do they keep throwing junk like that at us? Simple. It works. Why do we fall for it? Simple. We would like to believe it could be done—that we could save while we spend. Think for a minute. What could be more wonderful to our blazing hormones? Most people only work to spend. When they do save, it is only to build up a stack of greenbacks so they can really do some damage when they spend. What then would be more wonderful than to be able to do both, simultaneously? They could spend a pile of money so that more money (that which they just saved by spending) would somehow roll in. This, magically, would allow them to spend again, producing a new chunk of fresh savings which could then be spent. (Get another shopping cart, hon.) Like a perpetual motion machine (which is also fictitious) they could just go on spending forever.

If you border on being one of the many "spendaholics" in this nation (and it is estimated that the numbers reach into the millions) let me pass on a suggestion. Cut down on your television viewing. What does TV have to do with spending? When you take a step back and face reality, there is one truth about TV that comes through distinctly. It is camouflaged, but barely so. TV is not an education medium. (It could be, but it is not.) TV is not an entertainment medium. It is not a relaxation medium. You may *think* you are relaxing or being entertained, but when it gets right down to it you are being sold! Television is an advertising medium pure and simple. And I am not just talking about the commercials.

Try it. See for yourself. Cut down on the TV viewing and you will notice many beneficial effects. There will be less tension in your home, less bickering from your children, and a host of other benefits, including much less impetus to go out and spend money.

PLUGGING LEAKS PAYS

Don't stand there staring at the horizon while your financial ship sinks beneath you. Instead, tune in to the truths of owning a tight ship. Identify and plug the leaks that threaten your financial stability. Replace the dreaming with these thoughts from President J. Reuben Clark:

> Anyone who lives beyond his income is inviting disaster. Borrowed money is not income. Borrowing on capital account, within your reasonable capacity to pay, may be sound, depending upon circumstances. But borrowing to live on is unsound, whether it be an outright loan or installment buying. We urge the members to be frugal, thrifty, industrious, temperate, saving, and to live righteously. (CR, April 1940, p. 14.)

THIRTEEN

THE WEALTH PLAN

PLANK NO. 4:
OWN A DEBT ELIMINATION PLAN

If there is any one thing that will bring peace and contentment into the human heart, and into the family, it is to live within our means. And if there is any one thing that is grinding and discouraging and disheartening, it is to have debts and obligations that one cannot meet. (Heber J. Grant, *Gospel Standards* [Salt Lake City: The Improvement Era, 1941], p. 111.)

Americans, whose forefathers fought and died for freedom, have grown fond of servitude. For many it has become a way of life. Indebtedness is bondage. That is not just melodramatic hype. Paying interest is a form of servitude, a relentless form. Many of our brothers and sisters in this generation will go to their graves never knowing the peace and joy of being totally, completely out of debt. Statistics show that the debt liability for most families in the United States grows annually.

Extricating yourself from that quagmire—the quicksand of high levels of debt—takes time, but it can be done. The sooner you resolve to do it, the sooner you are going to know financial freedom. Do not procrastinate. Liberating yourself from debt requires more time and effort than most people realize. They do not fully comprehend that reality until they begin to actually make the attempt. Then they come to appreciate Mohandas Gandhi's astute observation: "Golden shackles are far worse than iron ones."

IT'S FAR EASIER TO BORROW THAN TO REPAY

I am not saying "Never borrow, under any circumstances," but I'm coming very close. There are some times and purposes when entering into debt may be justified. Getting a college education or purchasing a home can be justifiable objectives for some debt accrual. However, even for worthy objectives, enter into debt cautiously, prudently, and modestly.

I have seen many young people stifle their destinies by over-mortgaging their future through excessive borrowing during their school years. With a little more sacrifice they could have lessened the debts they undertook in the first place. Their future would have been brighter, and their prosperity would have come sooner and been more substantial in the long run. Some people accrue so much debt in their college years that they are playing catch-up for the rest of their lives.

The same principle holds true with home mortgages. Do not stretch yourself to the maximum and "grow into your house and payments." Paying interest does not build equity. Run (do not walk) from the financial advisors who tell you large mortgages are a good idea because Uncle Sam will allow you to write off a chunk of the interest.

Home equity loans are generally bad news in the long run. I have heard the Brethren—in solemn assembly, no less—counsel the Saints to shun them. It is not wise to fritter away the equity in your home. Instead of delaying it, you should be trying to accelerate the attainment of a mortgage-free roof over your head. Some rationalize, saying Uncle Sam gives them a break on their taxes. Even if Uncle Sam would let you write every last cent of mortgage interest off your taxes, not just a percentage, that still would not compensate for the lack of the peace of mind that comes from owning the most important material asset you will ever have: your own home.

HOW MUCH IS TOO MUCH?

This advice, I realize, may be arriving "post disastrum" (fictitious colloquial Latin is my sub-specialty). If you *know* you are in deep water in terms of debt, you must either embark on an immediate and undeviating course of debt elimination or deal with bankruptcy. Recommendations regarding both of these options will be discussed later in this chapter. If you are not sure about your debt situation, not certain how much debt is too much, here is a rule of thumb upon which to make a judgment.

Over the years, lenders have employed a simple guideline for evaluating risk levels. They calculate a "debt-to-income ratio" for the hopeful borrower. (This is why borrowers must submit those revealing confession sheets filled with personal disclosures known as financial statements.) The debt-to-income ratio serves as a meter to measure the borrower's financial buoyancy. This ratio is easily calculated. To arrive at your own, follow these simple steps:

1. List All Your Debts

Make no exceptions and do not fudge. List them all. You want to clear the table and remove every legal lien on your balance sheet and on your soul. There is more than meets the eye going on here. Debt has spiritual implications as well as financial. Later in the book this point will mean more than it does here.

Do not include regular monthly necessities, like food and utilities. Yes, you pay them monthly, but you do not pay interest on them. Furthermore, the amount you pay for food is discretionary and not a fixed contractual amount like a car payment. That is part of the point. You have monthly necessities and if, in addition to them, you have obligated yourself to a lot of other payments, you have very few dollars left over. If there is no reasonable place to fit another payment into your budget, a lender will not lend.

Most home payments include not only principal and interest but taxes and insurance as well. If your mortgage payment does not include all of those figures, add them to your mortgage payment amount. They are obligated mortgage-related expenses and must be considered part of the debt picture. If you are renting, do not include your rent on the list. We'll deal with that issue shortly.

2. *Determine Your Monthly Debt Payment (MDP)*

Once you have listed all your debts along with the monthly payment amount in each case, total the payment column. The total of all payments for all your debts is known as your Monthly Debt Payment, or your MDP.

3. *Determine Your Debt-Income Ratio*

Now divide your MDP by your monthly net income. "Net income" is all earned income immediately after governmental deduction but before anything else is subtracted. The answer you derive is a percentage or ratio called the debt-to-income ratio.

$$\frac{\text{MDP}}{\text{Monthly Net Income}} = \text{DEBT-TO-INCOME RATIO}$$

Example

Total MDP = $800

Total Monthly Net Income = $2,000

$$\frac{\$800}{\$2,000} = .40$$

Thus, your Debt-to-Income Ratio = 40%

Lenders have a standard ratio for *total* debt. Most lenders start backing off when the percentage of all debts (including the mortgage payment) falls in the neighborhood of 40 percent of the monthly *net* income. People in that position are a poor risk, because their discretionary dollars are severely limited. They are headed for Default City.

Accordingly, if you are not presently paying on a mortgage—that is, you are renting or have your home paid for— your debt-to-income ratio should not be over 15 percent of your net income. Compute your own ratio. If your debt-to-income ratio is above 40 percent (15 percent if you are renting), you are skating on thin ice. Reason and prudence beg you to lower your debt; and I am asking you to aspire to having no debt at all!

THE DEBT ELIMINATION PLAN

The following Debt Elimination Plan is tried and proven. It is straightforward and unambiguous. Once you have mastered the first two steps of the Wealth Plan—that is, you have (1) committed yourself to the Accumulation Mind-Set; and (2) you have mastered a monthly savings habit, paying yourself at least 10 percent per month—then you are ready to embark on the Debt Elimination Plan. It has subtle beginnings that gradually but steadily increase in potency, with remarkable results.

Right now you are obligated to pay a certain amount each month to your creditors (your MDP). Under the debt elimination plan this amount is going to remain unchanged throughout the process. Following the steps I am about to outline you will be able to pay off large chunks of debt without drastically impacting your monthly budget or having to increase your income:

1. Accrue No More Debt

NONE. From this point on, deficit spending is not an option. Be tough. Live within your income.

2. Set a Specific Debt Elimination Goal

Start with your debt-to-income ratio. What would you like that ratio to be? You may choose any percentage between zero and 40 percent. I recommend it be not more than 25 percent. In fact, I would like you to consider totally debt-free living.

3. Use Debt Service Money Exclusively for Debt Elimination

You will achieve your goal by using the money presently going to your creditors. As, one by one, you pay off your debts, more and more money will be "freed up." The "freed" money should stay in the debt elimination program until you have reached your goal. The power in the plan comes from using the freed money to accelerate the rate of repayment on your remaining loans.

THE STEPS IN THE PLAN

Now comes the implementation of the plan.

1. List Debts from the Smallest Balance to the Largest

Return to the Debt Schedule, or your list of debts. The debts have been listed in no particular order. Now reorganize them on another list, from the smallest balance to the largest.

2. Divide Your Savings Plan

If you have a high debt-income ratio (35 or above), you will need to modify your savings commitment temporarily. If you can avoid this modification, do so. However, if you are stretched to the hilt as it is, you will need to divide your monthly savings amount in halves. One half (or 5 percent of your net monthly income) will still flow into your freedom reservoir. The other half will be used to accelerate debt elimination. Although you slow down the growth of your savings for a time, you are better off by eliminating high interest payments. At this point that will be your best investment.

3. Pay Off Your Smallest Debt First

Begin eliminating your debts one by one, focusing on the smallest debt first. Irrespective of interest rate, payment amount, or any other consideration, attack the smallest balance first. The purpose is to eliminate one demand from your debt service and one worry from your mind as soon as possible. It also frees up some capital (not to mention the escalating cost of an envelope and one postage stamp).

On all but the smallest debt, pay the minimum monthly amount necessary to keep the account in good standing. On the smallest, pay not only the required payment, but also the 5 percent of your net monthly income. Shortly, you will have paid that debt off, and will have liberated some capital. At first, the plan will look like this:

Debt Elimination Plan

1. Debt 1   Regular Payment + 5%
2. Debt 2   Regular Payment
3. Debt 3   Regular Payment
4. Debt 4   Regular Payment
5. Debt 5   Regular Payment
6. Debt 6   Regular Payment

4. Roll All Freed Money Onto Debt 2

With your first obligation out of the way, roll that money onto the payment of the next debt on your list (Debt 2) along with the additional 5 percent, until that debt is paid.

2. Debt 2   Regular Payment + D1 + 5%
3. Debt 3   Regular Payment
4. Debt 4   Regular Payment
5. Debt 5   Regular Payment
6. Debt 6   Regular Payment

5. Continue the Process Until You Reach Your Goal

With the erasure of each debt, *all* the freed money is rolled onto the payment of the succeeding debt. The process continues until you have reached your debt elimination goal. Each time one debt is eliminated, the process accelerates a bit. What begins as a trickle soon becomes a stream and eventually a torrent. By this simple and reasonable technique, hefty amounts of debt can be expeditiously requited.

ANOTHER APPLICATION OF THE SUCCESS FORMULA

Previously I recommended a simple success formula that produces remarkable results:

> *CHALLENGE* yourself.
> *MEASURE* yourself.
> *SURPASS* yourself.
> *REWARD* yourself.

This same formula will pay major dividends when applied to the Debt Elimination Plan as well. Predetermine a few intermediate goals and establish an appropriate reward for each milestone.

In the case of the Debt Elimination Plan this incentive-bonus system is even more crucial. I have observed a number of households working toward debt elimination who started well and kept things going for a time. Then (and, interestingly enough, it was often just before paying off a major debt) they lapsed into a splurge mode again and marched backward a few paces. The reward system provides a way of avoiding that pitfall. Tie an exciting, appealing reward to the elimination of each creditor. That will get you past the "almost there" splurge syndrome.

To fund your milestone bonuses, allow yourself a little latitude with the "freed" money. This differs from my recommendation in regard to the Savings Plan. When you have completely, totally paid off one of your major creditors, especially if this has been a rather large debt, take one month off the debt elimination quest. The month after you have paid off the debt, take all of the "extra" money you have been using to pay off debts, and do something fun with it.

You may not be able to do much when you reach the first milestone or two, but that will change. As, one by one, your creditors are eliminated, the "extra" money available will increase nicely. Down the road a little you will have a fairly tidy sum with which to reward yourself.

A WORD ABOUT BANKRUPTCY

Some people who read this book may be in such painful
financial straits that it is virtually impossible to get themselves
out. For those who have never been in such a predicament, it is
easy to pass judgment. To those of us who have been spared
such anguish I say: "Count your blessings. Perhaps there, but
for the grace of God, go we all."

There are many fine, honest people who through no egre-
gious sin on their part find themselves trapped in a bed of
financial quicksand. If you are one of these, this is what I have
to say. We live in a great land. There is an inspired system of
laws which provide liberty and a reasonable degree of justice
for all. (Things are not perfect in the USA, but they top anywhere else on earth.) Within the framework of the law, there
exist legal and just provisions for debt relief. True, there have
been abusers, but not everyone who seeks protection under
those provisions is a criminal or a deadbeat.

In the Church we have been advised to avoid bankruptcy.
Yet when there is absolutely no other route, one might have to
proceed under the guidance of sound legal counsel. Bankruptcy laws are enacted, in my opinion, precisely for people
who have sound moral fiber but who have no other reasonable
alternative by which to end their monetary nightmare.

Often it is difficult to even obtain the facts upon which to
make the decision. People hesitate to consult an attorney when
they are in deep financial distress, because the last thing they
need is another bill to pay. I am not trying to give anyone's services away, but there is another small ray of good news. The
attorneys who specialize in bankruptcy law usually have a policy of offering, free of charge, an initial consultation. They will
listen to your story and describe your alternatives. You do not
incur a fee until you employ their services to enact one of the
alternatives. (Obviously, verify before you make the appointment that a free consultation is the policy of the attorney you
select.)

Despite all the negative lawyer jokes, the majority of
lawyers have a heart, and those who specialize in this area of

the law understand your predicament. I would recommend that you get two opinions. If you hear the same recommendation from two experts, you pretty well have your answer. It is important to know that there are different degrees of bankruptcy. Frequently referred to as chapters, each has its separate provisions and limitations. Chapter 7 is full-blown bankruptcy, while Chapters 11 and 13 are "partial bankruptcies," allowing you different ways of getting back on your feet without losing all of your assets.

Only you can decide what is right and what is wrong for you. It's a significant decision, and you must consider it prayerfully. There are serious ramifications—the blemish on your credit record, for one. As you study it out in your mind, you will know whether it is a morally and spiritually acceptable route for you.

FORECLOSURES

My philosophy regarding foreclosures is similar. Submitting to a foreclosure is not necessarily a flagrant moral transgression either. Sometimes, even for responsible people, there is no other reasonable alternative. Again, consult your conscience and counsel with the Lord before you decide. Only you can say whether it is legitimate or merely an expediency to avoid discomfort.

Keep in mind that on the deed or in the contract—the instrument you signed to begin the deal—your creditor agreed to accept certain remedies in the event of your failure to uphold your side of the agreement. The creditor agreed to that option at the outset. It is not unethical or immoral to let him or her exercise those options. They may not be pleasant for either one of you, but there is nothing improper or underhanded about letting them act within the provisions of the agreement. Know this, however: The law is on the creditor's side in such a case.

Responsible communication on your part can help in many cases. Most people are fairly reasonable and understanding, and sometimes things can be renegotiated. The point here is to seek out all your options before you finalize a decision. Enduring a foreclosure also has its consequences. It will blemish your credit rating almost as severely as a bankruptcy. In fact, in some cases it is considered worse.

ABOUT CREDIT RATINGS

The foregoing leads us to a discussion of credit records and credit ratings. The first thing to have clear is that a spotless credit rating is a valuable asset—one to be achieved and preserved. If you have a strong credit rating, it increases your financial options. If you have a good credit record, keep it that way.

For those of you who are debating alternatives such as foreclosure or bankruptcy, first know this: Blemishes on your record linger. They will be there for ten years. That is not the end of the world either, but you will live with that record, at least to some degree, for the next decade.

Before moving on, let us deal with the issue of credit repair agencies. I refer to the firms who claim to be able to clear your record. My advice is that you do not get involved with them. There is nothing they can legally do for you that you cannot do for yourself. If the items on your record are incorrect, you can rectify the situation by written documentation through the creditor who made the report or with the credit bureau itself. You do not need to pay a third party to accomplish that. If the information is correct, there is no legal way to expunge the blemish.

REBUILDING YOUR CREDIT

If your credit rating is defaced and imperfect, all is not lost. You can get yourself back into fairly good terms with the world in about two years. Here is how.

1. Establish Unwavering Discipline in Your Life

Until you get some self-discipline established, a poor credit rating can actually be a blessing. Easy credit has been your downfall. Having no other alternative but "pay as you go" may well be the beginning of a cure for your disease.

On the other hand, once you have overcome this weakness you must demonstrate that fact by living within your means and paying every bill promptly. As you try to reestablish your credibility with the world, any flaws here will be lethal. Stay current and pay on time!

2. Own a Savings Plan

Establish a savings account and add to it faithfully each month. That record in itself is something you can use to demonstrate to your banker that you have corrected your course. However, it is also a means to accomplish something even stronger, a passbook loan.

3. Obtain a Savings Passbook Loan and Repay It

Once you have accumulated a decent sum in your savings account you can obtain a loan, using that money as collateral. This is called a "Passbook Loan." Suppose, for example, you have $1500 in your account. You could borrow $750 with little or no questions asked. You would be giving your passbook to the bank in exchange for the loan. Until the loan is repaid, you would have no access to any of the money in your savings account. The bank would be willing to make the loan despite your past record, because there is absolutely no risk involved. If you fail to repay the loan, they will take the money out of your savings account.

Terms and conditions for such loans vary, so shop around. If you are climbing out of a bad credit situation, ascertain this information before you decide where to open your savings account. You must get your passbook loan from the same bank where you have your savings.

Obtain the loan and then make your payments flawlessly. Make sure each payment arrives a day or two ahead of the deadline and continue this practice for six to twelve months.

You have to allow enough time for this to show up on your credit record. As you go searching for terms and conditions, make sure the bank reports regularly to a credit agency. This is the entire reason why you are going through this whole scenario. It will do you no good if it is not reported.

Once you are sure your performance has been reported and now appears on your credit report, pay off the rest of the loan early. Then repeat this process with another bank. If you can afford to do so, you might want to be applying this procedure in two different banks, simultaneously. Don't strap yourself, obviously. Use your head, but the more entities that are reporting your good performance, the better.

4. Obtain a Credit Card

In the very same way you obtained your passbook loan and for the very same reasons, most banks will issue you a credit card. The credit limit will be a significant amount below the balance in your savings account.

Use the card for a few purchases each month. It is imperative that you do not exceed the limit and that you pay the entire balance off each and every month. A clean payment record on a major credit card is one of the fastest ways to reestablish your credit rating, because it gives you a broadly based credit standing.

5. Monitor Your Credit Record

You cannot afford another blemish on your record. From this point on it must be flawless. It is amazing how often mistakes are made on credit ratings and someone else's glitch winds up on the wrong record. The similarity in names, transposed digits on a Social Security number, or any number of other errors can occur. Keep an eye on your record. You have the legislated right to know what your record is, who has requested information from your file, and so forth. Exercise that right. Look in the yellow pages under the heading, "Credit Reporting Agencies." Call up one or two of the larger ones and get the information on how to monitor your status. Then do it, regularly. TRW Credit Data and CBI/Equitax are two of the largest systems nationwide. Following these suggestions, you can get yourself into a fairly good credit status within two years. When you achieve it, keep it!

FOURTEEN

THE WEALTH PLAN

PLANK NO. 5:
OWN A MONEY EXPENDITURE PLAN

Live strictly within your income and save something for a rainy day. Incorporate in your lives the discipline of budgeting that which the Lord has blessed you with. (L. Tom Perry, *Ensign*, November 1995, p. 36.)

Some people don't like to say dirty words. Some people don't like to hear dirty words. Some people don't like to read dirty words. *Budget* is *not* a dirty word. This is stated "tongue in cheek" because so many of us experience severe power outages when we hear the word *budget*.

In my seminars I have a way of getting around this mental blockade. I announce, "Wealthy people have mastered a money expenditure plan." The audience is momentarily thrown off balance while the real meaning of the phrase "money expenditure plan" sinks in. During that interval of stupor they write the "principle" down. Many actually seem quite impressed with it—it sounds so sophisticated. It isn't until they have opened their minds a bit, wondering exactly what I mean, that they discover the punch line. But that's the key: they open their minds.

If you are one of the thousands of people who have tried a budget and have only succeeded in discovering the depths of frustration, take heart; there is hope. I understand. I have been there too. The good news is that there is an answer. After a lot of pain and a lot of frustration, I finally discovered a few things that have made all the difference for me and my household.

The initial step is mental. You absolutely must first accept the idea that a budget is not optional. There are two important reasons why. First, it is the quickest way. (Nothing will expedite the accumulation of piles of money faster.) Second, it is the only way. (Remember, people who lack self-discipline, even if they fall into a large sum of money, do not—cannot—hang on to it.) Besides, a budget does wonders for your self-esteem and confidence, as well as for your pocketbook.

Mental barriers in regard to budgets are not in short supply. An array of decrepit excuses abound. Let us briefly examine the more common rationalizations about budgets.

MISCONCEPTION NO. 1: A BUDGET IS SLAVERY

"A budget is slavery in print. It robs me of my independence. I don't want to be bound to some piece of paper. I want to be free to spend my money how I want, when I want."

REALITY: A BUDGET IS THE DOOR TO FREEDOM

Be careful of what is labeled "freedom" and what is labeled "slavery." People who fall away from the gospel use the same rationale. There are serious overtones to consider. I have never yet heard an addict who did not say he or she wanted to be free—left alone to live life as he or she pleases. Addicts always, and emphatically, demand their *freedom*. It is a tragic misuse of a sacred concept. The hue and cry of the morally anemic is that adherence to standards is slavery. They delude themselves with self-indulgent rhetoric about devotion to personal liberty. They claim their lack of compliance is actually the manifestation of something much higher and more noble—an all-out abhorrence of slavery.

Addicts have bad habits, and there are all kinds of addicts. They only differ in which bad habit they prefer. Spending without planning is a bad habit. People who do not want to be "slaves" to a rational monetary plan of their own making are really saying that they would rather be "slaves" to their excuses *and* to their debts, bills, and overspending habits.

The reality is that it is not possible to achieve financial freedom until you are able to live on less than you make, separate needs from wants, vanquish your debts, and build up a pile of surplus cash. And it is *very* difficult to do that without a clear written plan.

MISCONCEPTION NO. 2:
A BUDGET IS FOR LOW-INCOME FUDDY-DUDDIES

"A budget is for nerds—the unimaginative—the kind of people that do not and never will have big money. When you have good money rolling in, you can spend all you want and you still have money left over. A budget is for methodical types who cannot see the big picture."

REALITY: A BUDGET IS FOR PEOPLE WITH VISION

Financial freedom is not a state of money. In reality it does not have all that much to do with amounts. It is, above all else, a way of living. It is a dynamic, abundant life that has, at its core, clear objectives and perspectives. People who achieve financial freedom have a vision. They know where they are going and how they are getting there. They are not dependent on luck or fortune. They are committed to cultivating and harvesting according to natural law.

Those who achieve genuine financial freedom have money—lots of it. They have lots of it because they do not let passion overpower purpose. (Do not these same truths apply equally well to our spiritual quest? I trust you are seeing the parallels all the way through this book.) They are in control. They do not allow impulse or whim to obstruct their achievements or to detract from their ultimate goals. They make sure their long-range objectives are the governing forces in their monetary affairs.

Thus they control the ebb and flow of their money with the instrument we call a budget. People with vision and purpose use a budget as the conduit that ensures that the money gets to the right places for the right results. If you truly want financial freedom, you do not leave it up to chance. You develop a pathway, then you walk it.

It is not possible to achieve financial freedom until purpose supplants passion. A budget is the key to that. It gives you the power to make monetary decisions with your head instead of with your hormones.

MISCONCEPTION NO. 3:
A BUDGET IS DULL. IT IS DRUDGERY IN PRINT

"Life on a budget is boring. It's a life of no hits, no runs, no fun. There is no room for spontaneity. I may never be rich, but at least I am going to enjoy what little money I get."

REALITY: A BUDGET IS GREAT SPORT

If you love sport and love competition, you should love the challenge of a budget. One of the reasons for the popularity of sports is that the results are generally unambiguous. In sports you keep score. The scoreboard tells plainly who wins and who loses. Feedback is instantaneous. Events in the game are immediately reflected on the scoreboard. Players have the ability to adjust and, thereby, alter the course of the game. A budget serves the same purpose. You can measure day by day your successes and failures. The feedback is instantaneous, giving you the ability to adjust and improve promptly. Thus, progress is accelerated.

The truth is that it is not possible to achieve financial freedom without a standard or without receiving feedback on your performance relative to that standard. A budget does that. Most important, (and better than most scoreboards) its message is preventive in nature. Through a budget, many disastrous decisions can be averted before they are physically enacted on the playing field.

A BUDGET FORM IS NOT THE BUDGET

I have talked with literally hundreds of people who are

attempting to achieve financial freedom without the use of a budget. When I inquire as to why, I hear universally the same response: "I've tried one and could not make it work." Probing a bit, I usually uncover more or less the same scenario. They talk of picking up some budget forms found on the stationery shelf at the corner grocery store—ones titled "Monthly Budget" or "Personal Budget." Devoting the better part of a whole hour, they proceed to dutifully respond to the various blanks with a monthly estimate that is usually a haphazard guess of what an "average month's" expenditure in the given category might be.

That done, they total the page. If it is in line with their net monthly income, they assume they have a budget. Their only criterion for this conclusion is that they are not in the red. The assumption seems to be that a budget is meant to just keep you from overspending. Thus they have built a road to solvency only. If things look like they will end up in the black, they are satisfied. They have a nice warm feeling in the heart, surmising that, at last, they are finally getting organized and disciplined. But their glow is short-lived.

Unfortunately, within the first couple of days their tranquillity is disrupted by the rude advent of an unexpected bill. The quarterly auto insurance premium arrives. Somehow, budgeting from the monthly perspective, they overlooked the fact that they have expenditures that come at regular intervals other than a month (like each quarter, or semi-annually, or annually). "Well," they think, "that is easy enough to fix." So they start a minor shuffling process that takes a little away from the clothing allotment and a little away from groceries and a little away from entertainment, and "presto-chango" they have pasted their little plan back together, and they are "still within budget."

Before long some other unexpected bill or necessity arrives on the doorstep, and the shuffling process commences anew. This time the shuffling reaches levels that would earn admiration in a Monte Carlo casino. Shortly thereafter (this interval ranges anywhere from two minutes to a couple of days), this fragile ruse is exposed for what it is and, with the combined emotions of frustration and relief, they hurl their "Monthly

Budget" at the neighbor's dog and are "finished with budgets!"

Now, if something akin to this Chaplinesque scene has been largely your experience with budgets, cheer up. There is hope. The fact is, you have never tried the real thing.

There are at least three fatal flaws in the above scenario:

1. They are budgeting in the wrong time interval.
2. They are beginning at the wrong end of the process.
3. They are not devoting enough time at the outset to really think and plan.

The adage holds true. Two wrongs do not make a right; and neither do three.

There are seven rules for successful budgeting:

1. *Define Annual Objectives.* Are you ready for a breakthrough in thinking on the subject of budgets? Here it is: A budget is not the brakes, it is the steering wheel. Too often we think of a budget as merely the way to stay solvent. We suppose that its purpose is to prevent overspending. But a budget is more than the road to solvency; it's the expressway to reach the specific goals and dreams you desire.

Start your budgeting process by deciding what you want to accomplish in the next twelve months. How much do you want to save? How much debt do you want to retire? What are the major purchases you want to make this year? Is this the year you're going to upgrade the computer system? Is this the year you're going to develop the backyard? This part of the budget can be fun, and I hope you will make it so.

2. *Budget from an Annual Perspective.* The tendency in budgeting is to look at things from a monthly perspective. People grab a monthly form and make projections on some "average month" that does not even exist. The problem with that approach is that not all months are created equal. A December is a whole different animal for most of us than, say, a March or an April.

Just as any good business does, a household absolutely must budget from a yearly perspective. Attempting to construct

a workable budget from a monthly perspective does not produce a clear vision of the whole territory. It leads to frustration
in short order. Look at the year as a whole and develop an
annual plan. It may take a little more thought at the outset, but
in the long run it is worth it.

3. *Use a Comprehensive Budget Guide.* You need to go beyond
the simple monthly form. You need a good format that will
guide you to really think things through. There are several
excellent software applications out on the market. The most
famous one is Intuit's product called "Quicken," but there are
several comparable programs that also are very good. You can
check your PC magazines and consumer guides to compare
their features.

4. *Verify the Facts.* Budgeters run into trouble when they
"just wing it" when it comes to projecting their expenditures. It
pays to know the past before you start trying to predict the
future. Go back to last year's check registers. Get a large sheet
of paper and make some columns on it so you can create categories of expenditures. Now team up with another person—
one of you will be the "reader" and the other will be the
"poster." Starting with the first check of the year, the reader
will read the payee and the amount, and the poster will post
the amount in the appropriate column. If the first check says
"Safeway," enter the amount in the grocery column. If the next
check says, "Texaco," enter the amount in the vehicle/trans-
portation column. And so on.

If you make a lot of purchases with a credit card, you will
want to use those statements to categorize where the money has
been going down that avenue as well. Once the poster gets the
categories defined, the poster can post about as fast as the reader
can read, and you will fly through your monthly check statements. It will only require about a half-hour and it's worth it.

5. *Categorize Expenses by When They Fall Due.* Some of your
expenditures come quarterly and some come annually. Take the
time to itemize what bills and expenditures fall in the year but
do not come monthly. Several expenditures come once a year,
every year, like Christmas, Father's Day, and Mother's Day, for
example. A good comprehensive budget guide will help you

think of and plan for these non-monthly expenditures as well. Do not ignore this rule; it's an important key to your budgetary success.

6. *Make Joint Commitments.* You and your spouse can be stronger as a team than you can be individually. Adopting a new habit that requires discipline is not easy for anyone. The process comes easier when you support one another. When it comes to budgets, united couples are far more successful than single individuals. One of the hidden blessings that can come is an increased degree of communication as well as greater trust and teamwork. There will come times when there may very well be just cause to deviate from your established annual budget. Let that always be a *joint* decision. Work as a team; and strengthen one another by constant communication and mutual commitment.

7. *Be Tough.* When you are tempted to break from your plan, rejoice. You have a singular moment in which to exercise your disciplinary muscle. In lifting weights in a gym, overcoming the opposing force (gravity) builds strength. The same is true of spiritual strength. Show the temptation who is boss. Every time you are enticed to deviate from your course and you reject the enticement, you grow stronger.

FOLLOWING CHRIST

It is true that self-preservation is the first law of nature, but it is not a law of spiritual growth. He who lets selfishness and his passions rule him binds his soul in slavery, but he who, in the majesty of spiritual strength, uses his physical tendencies and yearnings, and his possessions to serve purposes higher than personal indulgence and comfort, takes the first step toward the happy and useful life. This truth was taught not only "in the Beginning" when the Gospel was first revealed to man, but also when the Savior began His earthly ministry. On the Mount of Temptation was enacted the first scene in the Christ's earthly drama of the abundant life. There He resisted the challenge to gratify His appetite; He turned aside the appeal to His vanity and pride; He scorned the bribe of

worldly wealth and power, as in spiritual victory He said to
the Tempter, "Get thee hence," and "angels came and minis-
tered unto Him." Only thus by the brilliant triumph of the
spirit over the flesh can we hope for a better world. (*See* David
O. McKay, CR, October 1940, p. 104.)

FIFTEEN

THE WEALTH PLAN

PLANK NO. 6:
OWN ONLY THE ESSENTIALS

Men must learn the relative values of things of earth and of spirit. To part with our earthly belongings seems to us to be a sacrifice—but sacrifice always begets blessings. Whoever lifts his affections above earthly things expands in spirit and begins to grow. Latter-day Saints . . . must be able to control and subordinate the love of earthly things if they are to rise to greatness. (John A. Widtsoe, Evidences and Reconciliations [Salt Lake City: Bookcraft, 1960], p. 283–84.)

Adam Smith, a respected economic authority of the eighteenth century, wrote a landmark book titled *The Wealth of Nations.* This book, now over two hundred years old, is considered to be the cornerstone of the free enterprise system. In that admirable work, Mr. Smith stated: "The real price of everything, what everything really costs to the man who wants to acquire it, is the toil and trouble of acquiring it." (*The Wealth of Nations* [New York: P. F. Collier and Son, 1909], p. 36.)

With all due respect, Adam Smith was wrong on this matter. Acquiring is merely the prologue, barely a snowflake in a Himalayan avalanche of expenses that ensue when one acquires a bunch of mortal possessions.

COUNT ALL THE COSTS

Possessions exact far greater expenditures from owners than the mere toil and trouble of obtaining them. As a proud owner, you are now responsible for care, maintenance, and upkeep. You must protect and preserve your treasure, otherwise all the effort expended to acquire it in the first place goes for naught. Acquiring something is only the wedding. Upkeeping and maintaining it is the marriage. And few live happily ever after.

You see owners wherever you go. They are the ones with their sleeves rolled up, perspiration pouring off their brows, straining to repair, refurbish, or restore some mute, inanimate, and ungrateful object. They stand there splattered with paint or grease, shelling out more cash to preserve what they shelled out cash to acquire. Sometimes it's difficult to actually determine who owns whom. The owner seems to be the one whose freedom and mobility have been diminished. It is the owner who devotes time before work, after work, holidays, days off, vacations, and retirement tending the possessions. It is the possessor who's huffing and puffing, vainly trying to forestall the ravages of gradual disintegration. The possession makes no commotion. It just politely goes ahead and rusts.

Possessions don't fret; possessors do. Owners are the ones who must superintend, the ones who must varnish things, lubricate things, sand and scrape, caulk and putty, prime and paint, and pay taxes on *things*. They are the ones replacing filters, changing oil, poring over incomprehensible service manuals—winterizing, summerizing, patronizing, and (at regularly specified intervals) replacing one or more of the component parts on and of . . . THINGS!

Hear it, o ye ends of the earth! *All ownership is a form of bondage.* I know you may think me extreme, but consider my point carefully. I might not be as loony as you think. How much of our life and creative genius is spent taking care of "stuff?" It goes beyond tragedy. Like a land war in Asia, it is a no-win situation. We owners are futilely trying to reverse the course of the irreversible. And we use up time and energy in the process—resources we will account for in our post-mortality interview with the Lord. I cannot picture myself being all that thrilled if the Lord sums up my life with the praise, "Well, Dennis, you sure took good care of a lot of stuff."

During his mortal ministry the Lord admonished His disciples to put their hearts on things that do not rust or corrode (see Matthew 6:19–21). In mortality, things do not stay neat, tidy, or new. They dilapidate. Dust they are and unto dust they are returning. The more I think about it, the more I think the Lord wants it that way. He wants us to see the worthlessness of mortal possessions. He wisely unleashed a mighty law of the universe in our behalf. It works relentlessly, never waning even for a moment. It crushes everything in its path and it is one of the most prevalent truths of mortality. Amazingly, the principle is only two words long: STUFF BREAKS!

It is an inexorable, unavoidable, undeterrable law pertaining to all mortal creations. Do you have stuff? All of it, at this very moment, is anxiously engaged in breaking down and coming apart. It is only a matter of what stage it is in. Do not underestimate the power of this relentless law. Think about it. Think before you go acquiring all that stuff. Take a look around; everywhere you go you see things falling apart. They are in an irrevocable process of decay, disorganization, and disintegration. Govern your life accordingly.

The point is clear: Owners are not as deliriously happy as non-owners think they are. They are walking around, muttering obscenities, with burdens of maintenance on their backs. Ownership means responsibility. When that responsibility is for something that is going irreversibly downhill, it is best to keep ownership to a modest level.

OWN THE ESSENTIALS; RENT THE ACCESSORIES

I am not saying that you should not own *anything*. I am not saying that you shouldn't own your home or a car or two, or some furniture or clothing. On the contrary, I am a vociferous advocate of home ownership. Very definitely: *Own your home!* Go all the way. Don't just be paying on it. Own it. Despite what tax advisors and financial planners will say, *retire your mortgage!* And whatever you do, do not *add* to your debt.

Get yourself into a nice comfortable home and get it paid for as soon as you can. And don't go on an ego trip here either. There are too many SITCOMs out there that are not very funny. (You know what SITCOMs are, don't you? Single-Income Two-Children Outrageous Mortgages.) They are not all that funny. There is a lot more to life than making an outrageous mortgage payment for thirty years. Your home should be your castle, not your dungeon.

The tendency to measure one's worth in the world by the size of one's house is really preposterous logic. Yet family after family stretches itself to the utter limits, endeavoring to pay for the largest edifice possible. It would seem that the goal of every American family is to have a house that is sooo big that every member of the family, armed with vacuum cleaner and dust cloth, could not cover the premises in a week even if they never stopped for breaks, meals, or sleep. They would all just collapse late Saturday night in physical exhaustion somewhere between the kitchen and the twelve-car garage.

No matter how plush, a prison is a prison. I know dozens of families who are in bondage to a huge house with its huge monthly payment, huge utility bills, huge property taxes, its huge insurance costs, and its gargantuan demands for upkeep and maintenance. Own your home, my friend; don't let it own you.

Ownership to a point is wonderful. I believe that ownership of private property is an essential component of free enterprise and prosperity. But just remember, ownership comes with a *continuous* price tag. So do not get carried away. Keep your balance and your perspective. Own what you *need*. Own some things that you *want*, too. But do not imprison yourself in the cares of the world. (See Mark 4:19; JST Mark 4:16; Luke 8:14; Luke 21:34.)

CHEAPER TO OWN THAN RENT?

Count costs, especially when it comes to toys, recreational equipment, and recreational properties. I love to go to Lake

Powell, that picturesque marvel on the border of Utah and Arizona. We love to go as a family for an entire week on a houseboat. There is something for everyone at Lake Powell. Swimming, fishing, water skiing, mud wrestling—whatever.

It is a carefree place for me. Parenting is easy there. I do not have to worry about every move my posterity makes. I can turn the children loose on the beach and they cannot fracture or destroy anything costly or expensive. My liability to property damage is minimal. I do not have to be constantly shouting, "Don't touch that!" or "Stop that!" or "Be careful, you might break . . . " or "Watch out, you are going to ruin the . . . " and so forth. I enjoy more peace when not trying to avert disasters by small unskilled hands. Consequently, I relax. My little ones can just roam and explore. They cannot sunder that sandstone or break the lake. They cannot even stain or soil it much. It is about as sandy as it is ever going to get. All we have to do is pick up and carry off the litter when we leave (and in that category we try to go the extra mile).

I can rejoice in my posterity without scoldings and warnings endlessly spewing forth from my mouth. I sleep; they play. Then we play together. We get sunburned, and sandy, and we build fabulous memories and bonds of love. I can do that because I am not preoccupied with property damage. I've seen parents turn into boorish wrecks because they just bought a beautiful luxury cruiser and have to protect it all week. (They'd have more fun if they underwent liposuction without anesthesia.) Those lovely boats, so cherished in the show room, become sources of anxiety and tension on the lake. The parents lose sight of their purpose for the family vacation in the first place. They start resenting every movement their children make. "Don't do that, you'll scratch the . . ." "Stop that, you'll tear the . . ." "Watch where you are putting your punch, you'll stain the . . ." ad infinitum (and ad nauseam).

IT'S MR. WEBB'S BOAT (PROBLEM)

So here is what I do. When I want to go to Lake Powell and spend a week with the family on a houseboat, I pick up the phone, call Mr. Del Webb's company, and make a reservation. I mail a small deposit to him and write a date on my calendar. I do not have to worry about tune-ups, or whether the battery is charged, or any of that rot. My only worry is whether or not last year's swimming suit still fits. (Hey, Wanda, where's the 145 sun block?)

When I arrive at Lake Powell, the friendly folks at the marina provide me with a clean, decently operating houseboat that is gassed and ready for loading. I do not have to drag it behind my car and pray that it stays there until I get to the lake. (I have a friend who was pulling his boat to the lake and had the shocking experience of seeing his boat pass him on the freeway.) My way is less exciting; I just have to steer the car I am riding in. I do not have to worry about the boat along the way, or even launch it when I get there.

I then spend a week enjoying Lake Powell with my family with minimal concerns about the wear and tear on Mr. Del Webb's houseboat. We are clean, responsible people, and my children are well mannered. We do not destroy the rented property, but even if we did, I wouldn't have to call Dr. Kevorkian. My worries and financial responsibility would not be overwhelming.

When our holiday comes to a close, we gather what remains of our belongings, thank the folks at the marina, find our car, and drive home. I do not have to vacuum the carpets, wash the boat, wax it, or even park it. I just have to leave it in the water, more or less by the dock there. If there are a few extra scratches in the paint, I don't fret, and Mr. Webb has not yet called to harass me about the condition of his boat. Furthermore, from that point on, all of the joys of ownership are Mr. Webb's to savor for the rest of the year. If that night an unexpected typhoon brews up and sinks that nice boat to the very bottom of the lake, such news won't even spoil my next nap.

AND IT'S NICE TO CHOOSE

We look forward to those vacations. They are cherished times. I love spending some of them, as I said, at Lake Powell;

but what I also love is to *not* spend some of them at Lake Powell and take off for Disneyland instead. I also love to just stay home with the family and support my children in their various hobbies and activities. Above all, I love being FREE—free to do what feels fun, right, and most desirable at the time.

I don't want to feel obligated or pressured by some toy or property that I bought! People who spend a large hunk of change on a boat or a cabin sense pressure to spend lots of time using those toys. The expenditure haunts them a little. They have all that money tied up in that cabin in the mountains. When they would just like to stay home for the weekend, they cannot quite bring themselves to do it. The obligation to their cheery little cabin plagues their conscience. You hear them snarl at their children: "Come on, kids. Get in the car. We're going up to the cabin to have fun," they growl (in their un-funnest voice). So they press a little, and go there when they would really rather stay home or go somewhere else.

Do not let your decisions about how to spend your time be driven by how you have spent your money. I don't know about you, but I want my free time to be *free* time.

DOLLARS AND SENSE

Even if you just look at it economically, let alone spiritually, many of our recreational purchases make little sense. A houseboat these days is not a small-ticket item (in case you haven't noticed). What does one pay for a houseboat these days? If you are talking about sleeping and handling a family as large as mine, you are not talking under $100,000. If I really get into the ego trip, it would not be hard to spend way over twice that much. To handle my family of nine with spouses and friends we are not talking about a canoe here. We are talking about Motel 6 on pontoons!

For the sake of example, let us say that you decide to buy a $125,000 houseboat. That is just the sticker price. Let us say that you, like most people, have to finance a major chunk of it. That adds finance charges and interest costs to your recreation tab. Next come sales tax and licensing. (Such expenses also have the

nasty tendency of rolling around annually thereafter, only this
time they are called property tax and license fees.) They are followed by insurance expenditures. Then comes the question of
docking or storage. (You don't just let the air out of a 50-foot
houseboat and put it in your pocket. And you certainly would
not want vandals to mangle your treasure.)

All of this is just a foreshadowing of what is to come. The
great law of the universe, Stuff Breaks, now comes into effect.
Your gorgeous boat begins a gradual but unmistakable (and
irreversible) voyage to rust, dilapidation, and disintegration.
Since you are the proud *owner* of all that, "all that" is now your
responsibility; and your time, your strength, and your pocketbook are the only weapons you have to counter it. You soon
find that this arsenal cannot match the opposing force; the disintegration happens no matter what. You cannot stop it. All you
can do by throwing copious amounts of money, time, and
sweat at it, is slow it down. (A little.)

If you add up the purchase price and all of the aforemen-
tioned insults to your estate and wallet, the cost of two weeks
at Lake Powell reaches incredibly staggering heights. Even
when you spread that expense over a twelve-year period (the
average life of a houseboat), it is absurd to say that it is cheaper
to own than to rent. In most cases it is astronomically more
expensive. Even if all the infinitely irritating expenses, worries,
and distractions were set aside, and only the principal was considered, the savings are notable when renting.

For example, let us say you had the cash ($125,000) in your
hot little hand to pay cash for a swell houseboat. Instead of
handing it to the boat dealer, you just rolled it into a nice CD
that would pay an annual interest rate of 5.5 percent (which it
would as of this writing). Your annual income on the certificate
of deposit would be about $6,900. If each week's rental at Lake
Powell cost $2,500, (which it does right now) you could get two
weeks for $5,000. Just the interest on your principal covers your
houseboat rental. In fact, you come out $1,900 ahead right
there, plus you still have your principal working to pay for
your vacations next year. If you saved the $1,900, you have a bit
more interest next year on top of the $125,000 principal and you

gain even more ground. In twelve years, your boat, if you own it, would be depreciated to salvage value. You'd have an old scow worth a pittance on your hands, and a file cabinet full of receipts. If you do not own it—merely rent it when you want— you would have over $145,000 and no ulcers. (Think of the money you'd save on Maalox.)

TO OWN MORE, OWN LESS

The essential point here ought not to be missed. The issue is not how much one can save or make by owning less, but what one can *do* by owning less. Our mortal span is altogether brief. What we do with our time as well as our money tells much about the true God we worship. The Nephites got into trouble when they set their hearts on "the vain things of the world" and you will too. Own only the essentials, and you will have more space in your heart for who and what really matters.

"And verily I say unto thee that thou shalt lay aside the things of this world, and seek for the things of a better" (D&C 25:10).

SIXTEEN

The Wealth Plan

Plank No. 7:
Own a Low Maintenance
Investment Plan

It would appear that the inquiring rich man had lived in strict conformity to the laws known to him, that he saw in Jesus a teacher who could direct him to the fulness of reward in the mansions on high, and that he erroneously supposed he would receive direction to conform to some ritualistic requirement of the law. He had not learned that the Lord requires the whole soul and that those who gain salvation must love and serve God with an eye single to his glory. Rather, good as he was, his heart was still set on the things of this world in preference to the riches of eternity. (Bruce R. McConkie, *Doctrinal New Testament Commentary*, vol. 1 [Salt Lake City: Bookcraft, 1967], p. 555.)

Few idols today are made of stone. They are made of other substances like cellulose, silicon, plastic, and aluminum. While we often shake our heads in disdain and disbelief at the idolatry of the ancient Israelites, we have become the most idolatrous generation the world has ever seen. How clearly Isaiah described us:

Their land also is full of silver and gold, neither is there any end of their treasures; their land is also full of horses, neither is there any end of their chariots:

Their land also is full of idols; they worship the work of their own hands, that which their own fingers have made. (Isaiah 2:7–8.)

We have so many attractive distractions in our world. Bombarded as we are with enticements from every side, it is no wonder that few of us emerge from the confusion with our priorities in order. Certainly one of our greatest challenges today is to surmount the deluge of decadence and worship the true and living God. Clearly our devotion to the Lord can be measured by how we spend our time and where we center our thoughts. President David O. McKay said: "Tell me what you think about when you do not have to think, and I will tell you what you are" (*Gospel Ideals* [Salt Lake City: *Improvement Era,* 1953], p. 401). I pray we all see the value of centering our thoughts on the Lord.

For this and other good reasons I emphatically advocate a low maintenance investment plan. We need and want our money to grow, but we want to accomplish that without exchanging our prospects of an eternal inheritance in the process. You are not financially *free* if you are constantly shifting investments or monitoring the Internet five hours a day, no matter how much money you have. Those who spend their life fretting about the timing of their investments settle for pottage. The Low Maintenance Wealth Plan will be abundantly successful and far less thought-consuming than most other approaches you can find. Where you invest is ultimately more important than when. And what you do with your time while the money is working matters even more.

Preparing for Success

When it comes to money or earthly assets, nothing is perfectly safe. No matter what you do—no matter where you put your money—there still exists the possibility of losing it. Banks, savings and loans, and credit unions have failed and people have lost cash. Insurance companies have failed and people have lost money. Retirement funds have been embezzled or so mismanaged that innocent people have lost their nest egg.

Stocks have become worthless; bonds have defaulted. Gold, silver, and diamonds can be lost or stolen. Cattle can die, apartments can burn down (I've wished some of mine *would*), governments and companies can muddle, go bankrupt, or be taken over. Even cash can be stolen, lost, or beamed to other galaxies by aliens. (Well, it said so in the *Enquirer*.) Bottom line: In the absolute sense of the word, nothing is absolutely safe. Investment implies risk.

Accepting that as a given, the question remains, "What do I do with my accumulating savings?" There is no one perfect investment. The antics of inflation markedly affect the appeal of any given investment at any given time. When the rate of inflation is increasing, tangible assets are advantageous to own. When the rate of inflation is declining, cash and cash equivalents are better. People who "play the game" flop back and forth with the oscillating swings of the economic pendulum. Here we are not going to "play the game," but we are going to be wise. We will adopt a less hectic strategy, one that creates strength, balance, and growth no matter what inflation may do.

Key 1: Get Strong and Unencumbered

When it comes to successful investing, some words of caution are necessary. A lot of people get into trouble because they launch into the world of investment prematurely. They get greedy, dive into speculation, get strungout, sell early, and lose money.

First, get strong and unencumbered. Call *that* your *first investment* if you wish. Implement the preceding planks in the Wealth Plan. Establish your discipline—live on less than you make, eliminate all debt but your home mortgage, and live by a solid money expenditure plan. Then you are *really ready* to soar. Having shown your mastery of the preparatory law, you are entitled to more light and inspiration. What greater financial advantage could you ask for than the Lord's guidance and promptings in your financial ventures!

The second blessing that comes from this key relates to patience. People who are impatient seldom prosper in the markets because most investments require a period of time to grow. That is why you want to be solid financially before you enter the fray. If you are in a hurry, hoping your investments will pay off quickly so you can pay your bills and head off a foreclosure, you are not going to make it. Every blessing is predicated on a law, and that approach violates a bunch of them.

Key 2: Determine Your Investment Horizon

The investment horizon is crucial. If you are reading this chapter lying in bed, half asleep, put the book down and go to sleep. Read this when you are fully alert, because what comes next is pivotal to your investment success.

The foremost decision—the one that drives everything else—is to determine *the length of your investment horizon.* Putting it even simpler, you must first decide when you want your money back. This decision precedes every other one and governs all subsequent decisions. Before you can decide where to invest, you must determine how long you can let the money work. For our purposes we are going to say if you need your money back in less than ten years, you have a short-term horizon. If you can let your money work for ten years or longer, you have a long-term investment horizon.

Definitions: Short-term Horizon = Less than ten years.

Long-term Horizon = Ten years or longer.

When you get down to investment choices there is ultimately a fairly finite list of categories. New twists crop up all the time, but they are, almost without exception, variations on old familiar themes. Based on Nobel Prize-winning research, focused on the performance of investment vehicles, a very important point comes to light:

The best performing investments for short-term horizons prove to be the poorest for long-term horizons. And vice versa.

When looking at statistics compiled by the best actuaries and accountants—Ibbotsen and Associates, and others of that stature—regarding the overall performance of investment vehicles, you discover something significant. The biggest risk factor for short-term investors is volatility—the rapid fluctuation in value. The biggest risk factor for long-term investors is inflation—the slow erosion of value.

Certain investments that have low volatility prove to be superior when you want your money back in a few years. However, over the long haul they barely keep pace with inflation. Numerically, you have more dollars, but in terms of spending power you have remained the same or fallen slightly behind. You must do better than that or you will never get ahead. At the same time, certain investments with moderate to high volatility generally out-pace inflation sufficiently to give you a genuine gain over a long period of time. After factoring inflation into the equation, these investments produce real gains in spending power, which is of course what we want.

Thus you must be careful to choose the right investment for your particular investment horizon. If you pick a short-term vehicle for long-term objectives, you will wind up with a disappointing result. Similarly, if you use a fairly volatile investment for short-term objectives, you stand to lose a chunk of your money. Investors who will just abide by that one simple insight prevent a host of calamities. Use short-term investments for your short-term horizon, and use long-term vehicles for your long-term horizon. Stick to that and you will rarely suffer any major disasters.

It is okay to have two horizons. In fact, most individuals *need* both. If you are just starting in life, you need both horizons. You need, let's say, some money for the down payment on your first home in four or five years. Put the money you are saving for that purpose into short-term vehicles, because your goal is less than ten years. At the same time, the money in your freedom reservoir will not be tapped for thirty years or more; so for that money you want a long-term investment vehicle so that you can knock the socks off inflation and come out ahead.

Even if you are in retirement or are on the verge of retirement, you need both horizons. Some of your money will be needed within the next ten years, and some of your money needs to be working its hardest for the latter part of your retirement, *after* the next ten years. Part of your money, the part you need currently, should be held in short-term investments, and the rest should be in long-term.

INVESTING FOR SHORT-TERM HORIZONS

In general, your best investment for short-term horizons is a loan. Not as the borrower, silly—as the *lender!!* You want to be the one sitting on the lending side of the table, contracting with someone reputable, allowing them to use your money for a while at a good, solid interest rate for your compensation. Here are three time-proven ways to lend your money:

1. Certificates of Deposit

They may not be too glamorous, but don't get too proud. CDs have a lot to offer an investor with a short-term horizon. A CD is a contract between you and a bank or credit union. You agree to deposit (lend them) an amount of money for a fixed period of time. For this guarantee the bank agrees to pay you a higher interest rate than you would receive in a passbook account. This is an incentive for you to leave the money untouched for the fixed period. You give up a little flexibility in exchange for a better return on your money.

It is, in actuality, possible to withdraw the money, but there is a marked disadvantage. In the contract you agree to suffer a "substantial penalty for early withdrawal." (Bernardo "The Hairy" comes out of the back room and punches your lights out.) The penalty generally amounts to the forfeiture of your interest. You can get your principal back at any time, but you will suffer the loss of your interest.

The longer you tie your money up with the bank or credit union, the higher the interest rate they will pay. Usually, for periods longer than one year, the incentive is not worth the restrictions, but that is not always the case. As a general rule of thumb, opt for short maturities (six-month or one-year) when interest rates are low and likely to be going up. Conversely, choose longer maturities (three-year or five-year) when interest rates are high and likely to be going down. The definition of "high" and "low" is somewhat arbitrary and you can set your own scale, but for CD purposes high means over 8 percent. Whenever you can make over 8 percent, guaranteed, with virtually no risk, like a CD offers, do not turn your nose up and sniff at it.

Never put your money into a bank that is not federally insured. Federally insured means an agency of the U.S. government, the Federal Deposit Insurance Corporation, stands behind all deposits of $100,000 or less. Even if the bank defaults, the agency stands behind your account and you will get all your money back. The same thing holds true for credit unions. The banks and credit unions that are not federally insured usually have a private insurer. Even if they offer you a better rate, you are wise to turn them down and go with the federally insured institutions.

If you decide to put a lot of money into certificates of deposit, I recommend that you divide your money into several smaller CDs rather than putting it in one large one. (The exception to this may be the fact that you can get a much higher rate for keeping it as one lump sum.) Let's say you have $50,000 you want to put into one-year CDs. Ideally, you would divide your money into five CDs of $10,000 each, with staggered maturity dates about two to three months apart. That way you always have a CD reaching maturity. If an emergency should arise you have unpenalized money available within a reasonable length of time. If you do not need the money as each CD reaches maturity, simply roll the principal and the accrued interest into another CD that will mature in a year from that date. In following this suggestion you will have improved the "accessibility" of your money.

2. Money Market Mutual Funds

Money Market Mutual Funds (MMMF) are convenient and

flexible and allow you to have ready access to your money while it earns a decent rate of interest. A MMMF (not to be confused with money market accounts from banks and credit unions) is a way of obtaining a rate of return comparable to a $1,000,000 certificate of deposit. In essence, you are pooling your money with other small investors to gain the same return the "big boys" get. That is why it is called a "mutual" fund. Such funds are administered by brokerage houses, and some are offered by the large fund families on Wall Street. You can go either way.

There are several advantages to money market mutual funds:

1. Higher Yields. MMMFs compound at least monthly and most of them compound *daily*. The money is invested in short-term loan instruments with very short maturities. These funds always outperform passbook savings by a good margin and usually compare favorably to the longer CDs.

2. No Fees. Ordinarily, MMMFs waive their fees, so you pay no fees (often referred to as "loads") going in or going out of the fund. With some of the funds, however, there is a fee on one end or the other.

3. Check-Writing Capability. Many MMMFs offer a check-writing option that allows you to write checks and draw from your fund as long as the check amount is $250 or more. You cannot use this for your household checking, but it is a great place for your emergency fund. This makes your MMMF even more liquid than a passbook and you make a lot more interest.

4. Immediate Liquidity. You can withdraw your entire fund, if you choose, at any time by simply writing out a check for that amount.

5. Safety. MMMFs are among the most stable and dependable investments out there. The risk is minimal, especially in the funds that specialize in federal paper.

Several types of money market funds exist. Each invests (lends) your money in a different category of short-term notes and paper. One type will invest only in corporate notes. Another invests only in federal government bills with short to ultra-short maturities, and others invest only in municipal instruments. Each may have advantages or disadvantages, depending on your situation. A broker will be able to answer your questions and discuss the pros and cons with you. Remember that money market mutual funds can be obtained from a brokerage house and are one of the products you can get from them that do not incur a fee.

3. Treasury Bills

Treasury bills, often called T-bills, are about the safest way you can invest your money. You are lending your money to the U.S. government, which is about as safe as it gets on this planet. For people in high tax brackets, and especially for those who live in states with high personal income tax rates (like California and New York), they offer the added advantage of being exempt from state and local taxes.

T-bills are issued in maturities of 13 weeks, 26 weeks, and 52 weeks. You buy them below the face value at what is called "the discount rate," and when they mature you receive the face value on the bill. When they are held to maturity your profit is the difference between the face value and the amount you paid for them. You can sell your T-bills before they reach maturity for whatever you can get for them, but in that case you often incur a second brokerage commission that hurts your profits.

There are two ways to invest in Treasury Bills. You can set up a "Treasury Direct" account, in which case you pay absolutely *no commissions*. If you go that route, you must start with a minimum amount of $10,000, so that may put this avenue out of range for a while. The second way you can invest in T-bills is through a broker. Commissions are quite modest— in the neighborhood of $5-$10 per thousand. Fees vary from broker to broker, so shop around. If you would like more information on how to establish a Treasury Direct account or on T-bills in general you can call (202) 874-4000.

SUBDUE YOUR PASSIONS

Unless interest rates have risen to atypical heights, or sunken to uncommon lows, the returns one receives on short-term investments are rather conservative. It is important to realize that and not disdain them. Taking a statistical overview, the returns will range from 4 to 8 percent. Considering the surety of the growth and the safety these vehicles offer your principal, especially when inflation rates are also modest, these are acceptable rates of return. Do not reject them in your pride or your greed for faster growth.

There have been rare periods of time when returns have been much higher and a few when they have dipped below that range. Such conditions are deviations from the norm and are not likely to last long. If rates of return on such conservative investments soar, take full advantage of those unusually favorable conditions. You may even wish to shift a significant portion of your long-term money into them. I would love to have, as many of us did in the very late '70s and early '80s, a CD that was paying 11 percent on guaranteed money in a federally insured institution. One would be foolish to go any other route. Most of the time, however, short-term vehicles will return about half that amount.

Prudence dictates that the precept mentioned earlier in this book become your governing value: The return *of* your principal is more important than the return *on* your principal. When you begin to lust a bit, wishing for rates of return that push the limits, watch out. You are approaching a line which, if crossed, will disappoint you. The Lord rewards discipline; he does not condone the unchecked expression of our hormones. He will not undermine His own plan, which confirms on every level of the law that clear-thinking discipline is the tactic that prevails.

SEVENTEEN

The Wealth Plan

Plank No. 7 (continued): Own a Low Maintenance Investment Plan

Instead of searching after what the Lord is going to do for us, let us inquire what we can do for ourselves (Brigham Young, JD, 9:172).

If investment returns of 4 to 8 percent do not send you into orbits of joy, and you say, "I've got to have a better return than *that*," you can do it. But you will have to shift your investment horizon and mean it. Returns of 10 to 12 percent are realistic—not in a short-term context but in a long-term picture.

Investing for Long-term Horizons

When you shift from a short horizon to a long one, you also shift your basic premise of investment; you shift from loanership to ownership. You want to own something that is going to go up in value, something that will out-pace inflation. Sounds easy enough, and famed political humorist Will Rogers made it sound even easier: "Take all savings and buy some good stock and hold it until it goes up, then sell it. If it don't go up, don't buy it."

So the concept is simple; but finding something to buy at a reasonable price that will just go up and up can be a whole lot trickier than it sounds. For example, the stock market tends to go up *over time*. The hitch is that it does not just go up and up and up. The stock market, on its way to up, goes through a good number of downs too.

The stock market and the American economy in general have had, and will continue to have fevers and chills. People who try to sell just before a chill and buy just before the next fever are humbled in no time at all. History shows, however, that investing for *long periods of time* in the stock market *does* prove profitable and up to now has soundly surpassed inflation as well. So if you are looking for returns greater than 8 percent, you have to own some of the American economy, and that means you must go into the stock market, and to buffer the risks involved, you must commit yourself to a *long-term* strategy.

Broad-Spectrum Mutual Funds

When it comes to a simple, low-maintenance approach, and one that allows you to own part of America's prosperity while buffering the risk, broad-spectrum mutual funds are hard to beat. Specifically, we are talking about the type of mutual funds that invest in stocks. These mutual funds, often called "stock funds" or "equity funds," have had an impressive success record over the past several decades.

There are two other main branches of the mutual fund family—bond funds and money funds. I will not spend much time talking about bond funds. Here is the reason: The only time that bond funds do really, really well is when interest rates are declining, which occurs infrequently and only for short periods of time. The rest of the time, bond funds are okay but never scintillating. When you look at them as long-term investments they rate below average. When you look at them for short-term investments they do a bit better than average, but not much. We mentioned money funds in the previous chapter.

Broad-spectrum mutual (stock) funds offer you a number of solid advantages for your long-term money. First, you enjoy instant diversification. If you buy one or two individual stocks, your profits rise and fall based on the performance and fortunes of those two companies. Your risk is higher. One of the most validated adages in investing is the three-fold recommendation: *diversify, diversify, diversify*. It is a sound recommendation. Since mutual funds buy stock in a bunch of

companies (an average of 90 to 150 companies), when you buy
a single mutual fund you have automatically diversified your
portfolio. That is the power of mutual fund investing; you
spread your risk over multiple entities.

Broad-spectrum mutual funds take that good idea one step
further. They not only invest in multiple companies but they
also invest in multiple *sectors* of the economy. By contrast, there
are funds that specialize. They invest in a "niche" or in a specific, narrow sector of the economy, hence they go by the name
"sector funds." Although they invest in many companies, they
invest in companies that all do about the same thing, and when
that industry prospers those funds really move up. When that
industry lags or falters, there are no other assets in the fund's
portfolio to offset the downturn, and the fund will struggle. So
sector funds are diversified in terms of the number of companies, but in another sense they are not diversified. They still
ride the fortunes of only one part of the economy.

Broad-spectrum mutual funds invest in America. Your
money is spread across the breadth of the economy. If one sector does poorly there are usually a couple of other sectors that
are booming, and overall you get good gains from your investment. Even in a so-called "general recession" you can expect
one or two areas of the economy to grow. One person's misery
can often be another person's good fortune, and that maxim
can work in your favor. Your fund may not be soaring, but at
least it won't be plummeting to the basement like an elevator
with a broken cable. Broad diversification buffers risk.

The second big advantage to mutual fund investing is that
you can expect attractive long-term yields. A historical
overview demonstrates the following significant points:

1. Over ten-year periods, stock funds always outperform
    bank products such as passbook savings accounts,
    money market deposit accounts, and certificates of
    deposit.
2. Over ten-year periods, stock funds outperform bonds.
3. Over 15-year periods, stock funds beat inflation by 7
    percent or more.

4. The longer you hold stock funds the greater the likelihood of earning compounded annual growth of 12 to 15 percent. Even holding stock funds for ten to twelve years has historically meant that you would average 10.5 percent per year.

Other advantages to mutual funds include low-cost professional management (you pay a small percentage of your account value to the person making the decisions about which assets are bought and sold), low-cost personal management (checking on your fund performance is quick and simple), modest minimums to start (many funds start at $250 or $500), and small incremental increases are allowed.

The final advantage to itemize is *liquidity*. Mutual funds are easy to convert to cash. A phone call or letter will do it. Most mutual funds are "open-ended," meaning that when you invest in a fund, the fund issues new shares. When you want to sell, the fund buys the shares back. No questions asked. You do not have to have, as you do with individual stocks, somebody willing to buy when you are willing to sell.

Let me conclude this overview of mutual funds by sharing, for emphasis, an important perspective from Peter Lynch, a well-respected Wall Street figure: "Nobody who needs their money in one or two years should be in stocks or stock funds. But if you have a long term investment horizon, a well-selected portfolio of stock funds is bound to prove a winner."

THREE CARDINAL RULES OF INVESTING

Before you go running off to invest in your first mutual fund let me share three very valuable rules. Even if you consider yourself a seasoned investor, you do well to remind yourself of these time-proven precepts:

1. Always Invest with Your Own Money

Borrowed money does not have the same meaning or value as earned money. You do not take the same pains to look before you leap, and that little less caution can be costly. People who invest with their own money tend to ask tougher questions, look a little deeper, and investigate a bit more thoroughly before they jump. All that bodes well for better results.

2. Always Invest Based on Your Own Knowledge

Before you put your money in any investment, become knowledgeable in that investment and that market. Although you may be revved up about jumping into mutual funds, you need to gain more knowledge in the specifics of how and when and why than this book can supply. Take some classes, read some books, gain knowledge. Do not, in mental laziness, turn your money over to a professional or an expert and say, "Tell me what to do." You are asking for trouble; it just won't work. Again, the point of life is to learn to be strong and independent. We should not expect to see dependency rewarded. If you expect to really succeed, you must take responsibility for your investments and investment choices.

3. Keep Total Control

Nobody will take care of your money better than you. Nobody will act in your best interest as consistently as you. The financial literature is full of sad articles, relating examples of people who turned the decision-making responsibility completely over to a "pro" they thought they could trust, and lost their money. It goes against all laws of prudence and judgment to think you can walk into a broker's office and say, "Here's my money. Invest it for me, and call me when I'm rich."

BROKERS AND ADVISERS HELP

None of what I have just said should be construed to mean that brokers and professional investment advisers are not valuable members of your team. They can definitely help you win the game, but you need to see yourself as the quarterback. You call the plays and run the game plan. Reputable professionals in the field offer many valuable services, which include their perspectives over years of experience (a key qualification to look for as you pick a broker); they are excellent sources of investment data and research reports, and they can render valuable assistance with tax and estate planning.

Pick your investment advisers as you would a brain surgeon—check their background and reputation among their colleagues. Do not rush the process. Ask around. Check with the Better Business Bureau about the company or firm. If your broker works for a large, established company, find out how long he or she has been with the firm. Find people with a proven track record. Talk to people who have used the adviser's services for several years. If they are still happy over a reasonable period of time, that tells you something.

One more thing may give you some comfort as well as guidance as you select a broker. Look for a brokerage which is insured by the Securities Investor Protection Corporation (SIPC). Similar to FDIC, this agency insures your account against loss, if the brokerage house should go out of business or become insolvent. Accounts are insured up to $100,000 in cash *and* up to $400,000 in other assets. You must understand that this "insurance" does *not* apply to the performance of the assets in your account. If you buy a stock and it goes down and you sell, you lose money. (I know of no insurance to cover the risk of investing.) Most brokerage houses—both full-service and discount—are insured by the SIPC, but it is wise to verify that fact before you elect to go with a given firm.

THE CALPURNIA PRINCIPLE

Here is one final thing about investment, and it may be the biggest key to your investment success. I have dubbed it the Calpurnia Principle. If you are familiar with Roman history, or at least William Shakespeare's rendition of it, you will recall the name. Calpurnia was Julius Caesar's wife. It was she who received the dark forebodings regarding Caesar's trip to the senate. Her dreams in the night were fitful and she awoke with a warning for her husband. She pleaded with him to forgo his appointment that day. Had mighty Caesar heeded his partner, he would at least have lived past the Ides of March, averting his assassination at the hands of Brutus and Cassius.

In any given partnership or marriage, one partner tends to take the lead in investment matters. There is nothing wrong with that. But for married people my firm recommendation is that, from this point on, you never proceed with any investment unless there is complete unity between the two of you, and that you make the decision a matter of prayer.

Keeping in mind that the second law of accumulation is, "Don't Lose What You Save," you will do well to "listen to your partner!" Time and time again I have seen grievous financial disasters avoided when this rule was observed. One spouse wanted to run headlong into a venture, while the other felt significant misgivings. In 99 percent of the cases the "mixed feelings" have been a warning. The couple has been spared by heeding them. The converse is also just as consistently true. I have seen serious financial debacles result when one partner has stubbornly pursued a hunch contrary to the strong misgivings of the other partner. There are exceptions to this rule, no doubt, but they are few and far between. I personally cannot think of one exception in my own experience or that of my acquaintances.

The bottom line: Work as a team and communicate—communicate with one another and with the Lord, and you will seldom go wrong.

EIGHTEEN

THE WEALTH PLAN

PLANK NO. 8:
OWN AN EXPANDING INCOME

Nor is it enough that the one get rid of evil. He must do good . . . He must cultivate noble sentiments by performing noble deeds—not great ones, necessarily, for opportunity to do what the world esteems great things, comes but seldom to men in the ordinary walks of life; but noble deeds may be done every day; and every such deed performed with an eye single to the glory of God, draws one that much nearer into harmony with Deity. (B. H. Roberts, *The Gospel and Man's Relationship to Deity* [Salt Lake City: Bookcraft, 1965], p. 197.)

The Abbotts are feeling great these days. Financially, they have never felt stronger. They have accumulated $35,000 in their savings account. This is the largest their reservoir has ever been. Their income is far from lavish, but they are living within their means and enjoying a respectable life-style. The future looks even brighter. They recently received an increase in their income and the prospects for future increases appear virtually certain. They feel solid.

The Babbotts are feeling uneasy. They are weighed down with financial concerns. They, too, live comfortably and prudently. However, their employment situation is unsettled. Their employer is cutting back drastically. There have been layoffs recently, and rumors abound suggesting more to come. The Babbotts have $135,000 in savings; but facing the specter of unemployment, they know their savings could disappear quickly. They feel vulnerable.

The Abbotts feel confident and positive with $35,000 in the bank. The Babbotts can hardly sleep at night with over three times that much. Moral of the story: Reservoirs alone do not provide financial security. Wealth is relative, and financial security has more to do with trends than amounts. Wealth is best viewed as a monetary *flow*—a complete watercourse *system*. It is not just the river, nor just the reservoir, nor just the dam. It is the entire system, rainfall to faucet, supplying a continual flow of the indispensable fluid that sustains life.

An effective, life-sustaining river system does not exist without a sturdy dam. This supplies control over the resource. In financial terms, the dam is your budget and your savings plan. It is founded on the bedrock of your self-control and discipline. Eliminating your debts plugs the leaks in the dam and solidifies the system's strength. If you do all that, you will get a reservoir. But wealth goes beyond that. When you have a well-constructed dam with little or no leakage, and a handsome reservoir filling in behind it, you are ready to go back and tend to the river. Once the control system is in place, then everything that follows depends on the measure of the river itself. Two things determine the flow of a river: the amount of rainfall and the size of the watershed. Increasing either one of these factors enlarges the volume of the river and the rate at which your reservoir fills.

RULES FOR A RIVER

Here are the three fundamental rules for creating a mighty financial river:

1. Labor at something you love.

2. Stay focused and invest in yourself.

3. Solve other people's problems.

Labor at Something You Love

Take this quiz:

1. When you are at work do you find yourself watching the clock?
2. Do you "live" for evenings, weekends, and vacations?
3. Do you tend to pursue exciting, even dangerous, hobbies?
4. If you inherited a fortune, would you quit your job?
5. If you knew you were going to die in three years, would you leave your current profession or occupation?

It doesn't take an Einstein to see where this quiz leads, but the implications are bigger than many people realize. Those who answer yes to these questions have a low likelihood of ever being a financial success. Worse than that, they are wasting their life. Forgive my bluntness, but if you are not engrossed by your life's work your dreams of a richly abundant income stream will not come to pass.

Many people think they will find happiness in leisure and recreation. Not so. Service begets joy, and fulfilling work is the elixir of life. Robert Louis Stevenson said, "If a man loves the labor of his trade, apart from any questions of success or fame, the gods have called him" (Bill Adler and Bill Adler, Jr., *The Wit and Wisdom of Wall Street*, 1985, p. 18). True, we need a share of diversion and relaxation, but study after study shows that people who love their work live longer, have less disease, and make tons more money. People who love what they do seldom have to "get away from it all." They're *doing* what they love to do, enjoying the hours of their life, instead of counting them. Even going on vacation is kind of a bother, because what they really want to do is back home. And because they love what they do, they do it well and unconsciously add that magical element called *quality* to their work.

John Serves

Sometimes it is difficult to describe, but people know value when they see it and they want it. They will even pay more money to get it. Many intangibles factor into the perception of value—things that are not even necessarily part of the product itself. Often it has something to do with the "personal touch" and extra effort when it comes to service.

I own a car. Generally it is a dependable car, but once in a while it needs some help. When it comes to repairs and maintenance, I want value. Maybe it is paranoia, but in times past I have felt ripped-off when I have had my car serviced. I had serious doubts about value; until I met John. Now, I have one less worry in my life. John repairs cars; and he gives value. I can feel it. This man conveys that "something extra" every time I take my car in. He is always smiling. Even when he has put in ten hours at work and you know his body is exhausted, you still see that smile.

You can tell he loves cars. You sense it when he talks about them. He bubbles over, relating stories and offering careful explanations (including sketches) about how my car is getting along and how I need to watch for this and that in the next five thousand miles or so. Sometimes I get the feeling John likes my car more than I do.

When my car needs help, no cursory "It'll cost you 350 bucks to get this one runnin' again, Mac," will do from John. No sir. John takes me right into the operating room. He wants me to get right under the car, poke my finger into the "blood and guts," so I can see for myself which part is broken. All the while he tells me about my options, whether or not a rebuilt part may do, what I can do to "get by for a while," and what will be the best long-term solution. I would never *think* of taking my car to anyone else. My friends feel the same way. We go only to John, because we want value; and we get it from John because he does not withhold service. He *gives* us service. We give him money in return. And the word gets around. Customers recommend their friends to John. John is getting rich. He likes that. But what he *loves* is helping people with their cars.

Stay Focused and Invest in Yourself

Once you have found your life's work, settle in and keep improving your skills. Take note of another key point from the National Science Foundation study on financial high achievers: "Your work is more likely to make you wealthy than any bet or investment you will ever make. . . . The most profitable place to invest surplus income is in the area which produced the income in the first place. . . . Any investment that helps detach you from work you enjoy and makes you anxious about the future [had] better produce a million dollar profit, because it is costing you the best chance you have, by far, of making a fortune." (Blotnick, pp. 5, 94, 134.)

Contemporary author Bill Copeland said, "If you chase two rabbits, both will escape." Concentrate on expanding the real source of prosperity, the talent, gift, or service you are best suited to render mankind. Journalist Walter Lippmann observed: "A man cannot be a good doctor and keep telephoning his broker between patients nor a good lawyer with his eye on the ticker." (*The Wit and Wisdom of Wall Street*, p. 52.)

I hope one of your life's goals is to become one of the very best at whatever you do. It needs to be a worthy pursuit, so it fosters continuous improvement and growth as a person. The qualities you develop as you stretch for excellence allow you to command greater income. You cannot demand or justifiably expect higher wages from your employer or from your society unless your contribution is expanding. This world is not fair in many respects, but I believe it is well nigh equitable on this point. Over the long haul, in the marketplace, value extended brings its just compensation.

Study your craft. The doorway to profitability and prosperity is knowledge and expertise. Your mind is what you offer the world. Educate yourself ceaselessly. Read. Study. Some of the best money you will ever spend will be on the development of your mind. In this information-intensive era we live in that is more critical than ever before. Education can no longer be viewed as an event or a stage of life that one passes through. It must be an on-going habit, an integral part of your life and lifestyle. The greater your mental powers, the greater your value to others and to the kingdom of God. This topic has clear temporal value with great eternal implications (see Proverbs 3:13–18). The wisdom of Brigham Young still rings through the years:

> We understand but a very few of the simplest and most self-evident truths and principles which govern and sustain us in existence as human beings, and all the rest which we have to learn is as great a mystery to us as the most intricate and delicate piece of mechanism is to the infant child. We need constant instruction, and our great heavenly Teacher requires of us to be diligent pupils in His school, that we may in time reach His glorified presence. If we will not lay to heart the rules of education which our Teacher gives us to study, and continue to advance from one branch of learning to another, we never can be scholars of the first class and become endowed with the science, power, excellency, brightness and glory of the heavenly hosts; and unless we are educated as they are, we cannot associate with them." (JD, 10:266.)

The time and money spent tinkering in the markets would return far greater rewards if instead they were invested in cultivating our minds and our abilities to serve other people. A part of your income must always go back into furthering your earning power. But it is well to remember that the learning Brigham Young spoke of is one investment that pays dividends both in this world and in the journey to come.

Solve Other People's Problems

You have heard it said, "Wealth went to that person's head." I prefer to think that wealth does not *go* to your head; it *comes from* your head. Wealth is ultimately a product of the mind. It seldom comes from physical labor. More frequently it stems from vision and creativity. Creative solutions to vexing problems are in high demand. They always have been and always will be. Anyone with the insight to come up with an invention, a service, or a product—something to ease pain, labor, or drudgery—has generally been financially rewarded. Advertisers have come to recognize that the clearer a product is aligned with the specific problem it solves, the better. Hence the success of products with names like "Easy-Off Oven Cleaner." Such a name doesn't leave much doubt about what the product does or why you might be interested in exchanging cash for it.

The simple truth is that human beings loathe exertion, despise problems, and abhor pain. They will avoid any one of these (or any combination thereof) with a vengeance. Whether that is good or bad is, for the moment, beside the point. The fact remains that anytime someone or something can reduce labor or the costs of labor there is demand for that service. People pay money to have their problems solved. They do it gladly. Perfect strangers will elatedly compensate you for solving their predicaments or easing their pain. This is the supreme law of temporal economics.

Calm, clear minds recognize that axiom and capitalize on it. If you want to expand your earning power, expand the vision of yourself in the role of problem solver. The grand question to ask is, "What problems exist in my profession or field of expertise? What problems can I help solve for other people?" Such inquiry triggers the creative juices, producing workable solutions that lead to demand for *your* service. Justly, the reward is proportionate to the magnitude of the problem. The bigger or more widespread the problem, the bigger the opportunity to profit by being the one to solve it.

Frequently the opportunity to serve comes cloaked in the disguise of "a problem." Most people do not look at life that way. They do not see problems as opportunities to render service. Instead they fret and cringe, lamely wishing the problem would just go away. Alert, composed minds see a problem as a chance to contribute, and they get to work. The first person to find a solution gets the larger reward. It seems to me to be a very just equation. You help others, you profit. The greater the service, the greater the reward.

When you are laboring at something you love, investing in your mind, and seeking solutions to other people's problems in the realm of your expertise, something significant happens to you. Your mind is capable of seeing things other people do not see. You heighten your awareness of needs and enhance the likelihood of receiving insights specific to your field of work. Strokes of genius, "lucky breaks," and ingenious breakthroughs don't just happen, especially when one of them results in substantial income. Somewhere along the line, someone has put in the hours and effort to obtain the inspiration. God is no respecter of persons.

With clarity and eloquence, President Spencer W. Kimball taught: "Work is one of the essentials to success. . . . Those tremendously useful men, those powerful and invincible men, Marconi, Edison, Orville Wright, Burbank, who sit wrapped in purple robes of creative genius, are simply men who are capable of striking reiterated blows. They are men who reached success because they subjected themselves to the fierce fires of intellectual and physical endeavor. Men never ascend to emi nence by a single leap or by growth overnight. Longfellow gave us this: 'The heights by great men reached and kept were not attained by sudden flight, but they, while their companions slept, were toiling upward in the night.'" (*The Teachings of Spencer W. Kimball*, ed., Edward L. Kimball [Salt Lake City: Bookcraft, 1982], p. 360.)

When you put forth consistent, righteous effort the Lord will not wait long before He moves to fulfill His promises. In effect, through diligence, service, and persistence, you expand your watershed and seed the clouds. Good things inevitably flow from that. Before you know it, rain is falling. Once it starts, it pours. The rainfall runs to the riverbed. Soon, what was once hardly more than a brook becomes a robust river, which in turn becomes a mighty torrent. Before long you have an income stream you can scarcely believe, and you will wonder where all that money was hiding during your years of struggle. Like an August thunderstorm, the downpour can come quickly and abundantly. Wealth does not take long to arrive, once you get your act together and demonstrate that you won't just consume your paycheck on your desires. You are never too old. It is never too late. Once the preparations are made, the rains will come.

NINETEEN

The Wealth Plan

Plank No. 9:
Own Freedom

And moreover, I would desire that ye should consider on the blessed and happy state of those that keep the commandments of God. For behold, they are blessed in all things, both temporal and spiritual; and if they hold out faithful to the end they are received into heaven, that thereby they may dwell with God in a state of never-ending happiness. O remember, remember that these things are true; for the Lord God hath spoken it. (Mosiah 2:41.)

Heavenly Father has commanded His children in many things and appended to some of these commandments certain promises and blessings. A vivid example comes to my mind due to a recent family experience.

About a year ago, our seventeen-year-old son, Timothy, was diagnosed with a large, invasive tumor in his head, an angiofibroma. I recall very well the thoughts that coursed through my mind and the wonderful spiritual assurance that entered my soul in the midst of those thoughts. That subtle impression, that divine influx of knowledge, was the foundation for me and all of my family as we passed through one of the trials of life.

The minute I realized that we were dealing with something very serious, possibly life-threatening, my mind ran to the ultimate question, "Is Tim going to die at such a young age?" As I mentally weighed that query, I thought about the life my son had been living. He was and is a wonderful son, never giving his mother or me a moment of concern, always a contributing, positive force wherever he went. He honored his parents and his family name. Furthermore, unlike many teenagers who find obedience to parental requests an irritation, one of Tim's singular traits was his willingness to obey his parents. Whenever he was asked to do something by Susan or me, there were no groans, no rolling eyes, no "Why can't somebody else do it?" It was always, "Yes, Mom; Yes, Dad."

At that moment, as I reflected upon his obedient ways, the goodness of his life actually elevated my concerns. I believe, you see, there is some truth to the old adage that says, "only the good die young." My first thought was, "Maybe Tim is one of those special ones who is not appointed to tarry very long. Perhaps he will not be with us much longer." Instantly, another thought entered my mind, something more than my own deliberations. This thought was transported by a conduit of spirit, confirming and reassuring even as it informed. Tim's most exceptional trait, his obedience to the commandment, "Honour thy father and thy mother," which had originated my concern, was also the very key to answering the question, "Is Tim going to die soon?" This great commandment has a promise attached to it! A wonderful, comforting promise to us at this moment! "Honour thy father and thy mother: that thy days may be long upon the land which the Lord thy God giveth thee."

Timothy had been obedient to a law with a promise, a specific promise, and God will not deny His word. Never. I knew at that instant, deep within my soul, that Timothy was not appointed unto death at that hour. Because he had been obedient to that specific law and others, he was entitled to and would surely receive the promised blessing. From that point on, my faith in the outcome was rock solid. I knew that if we did all in our power to study this thing out, search for the right doctor or team of doctors, leave no stone unturned, Heavenly Father would guide us and He would do the rest. Everything beyond our power, necessary for Tim's successful cure and recovery, would be granted.

And it was so. We did our part, an amazing team of surgeons at Barrow Neurological Institute did theirs, and the Lord did all the rest. Tim enjoys a full and complete eradication of the tumor. There is hardly a visible scar on his body and he has not one limitation or disability as a consequence of the tumor or the treatment to resolve it.

LAWS WITH FINANCIAL PROMISES

My faith in the Lord and his infallible promise-keeping grew a great deal through that experience. I also know and testify that there are other commandments with other promises which are just as sure. Permit me to share with you some of the laws which have that blessed intermingling of temporal and spiritual rewards.

"Remember the Sabbath Day, to Keep it Holy"

The Lord's promise in olden times regarding the Sabbath has been renewed in our dispensation. To the children of Israel in ancient times He promised to send rain in due season, enrich them with yields from the land and the trees, help them vanquish their enemies, bless them with peace and safety in their land, multiply their numbers and establish His everlasting covenant with them. (Leviticus 26:2–13.) "And I will walk among you; and will be your God, and ye shall be my people" (Leviticus 26:12; see also Isaiah 58:13–14).

In some of the most eloquent prose in modern times, the Lord reaffirms these promises. I invite you to read and savor the expansive promises extended in section 59 of the Doctrine and Covenants, verses 9–21. Among these joyous words we find, "inasmuch as ye do this, the fulness of the earth is yours" (D&C 59:16). Further on, the Lord makes the intention of Deity to make His people wealthy unmistakable, if they will but receive the wealth in gratitude and use it for worthy purposes (D&C 59:20–21; see also 78:19). Again, when we are prepared to receive, the abundance will come.

Clearly one of the preparatory requisites is meticulous observance of the Sabbath law. That Sabbath law has full-week conditions. It's not just about Sunday. "Six days shalt thou labour, and do all thy work." Just as important as keeping the Lord's day free from toil and the cares of the world is the command to work diligently the other six days. Hit it with all your might for six days. Stretch your mind and your muscles. "Cease to be idle . . . cease to sleep longer than is needful; retire to thy bed early, that ye may not be weary; arise early, that your bodies and your minds may be invigorated" (D&C 88:124). All these things pertain to the Sabbath law. Daily, part of our strivings need to be in things spiritual—scripture study, mighty prayer, and a time for meditation. These practices add to our power to perform our daily labors well and righteously, and to stay in communication with the Lord. Then on the Lord's day, the Sabbath, we consecrate the *whole* day to that communion.

The Sabbath law requests more than cursory effort. The rest we seek on the Sabbath is not a six-hour nap but rather the peace and rest that comes from being immersed in the light and power of the Spirit (see D&C 84:24). The Apostles and prophets of this dispensation have repeatedly declared in detail and plainness elements of keeping the Sabbath law. If needed, refer back to recent conference addresses and refresh your vision. We are not keeping the law by merely attending a block of meetings. I remember hearing a brother remark to his bishop, "I want you to know, Bishop, that I don't even think of going hunting on Sunday, until I've been to my meetings." (And he was serious.)

In Father's kingdom there are degrees of glory because among His children there are degrees of obedience. To obtain the higher degrees of glory one must live the higher dimensions of God's laws. If you think you have the law down cold, that is the surest sign that you don't. There is no end to the upgrading we can make to this law or any other in our lives. Prayerfully introspect for a bit and you will hear the Spirit whisper what is next for you. Follow that personal commandment, and keep it personal. Do not expect everyone to be at the same level. They are not. Upgrade your own observance of the Sabbath law and rest assured the promises will be fulfilled upon your head. You will experience greater blessings, one of which will be increased prosperity in temporal matters.

"The Fast That I Have Chosen"

Among the writings of Isaiah we find precious passages regarding some of the higher elements of the law of the fast. In chapter 58, verses 3–12, the Lord reasons with His people. Stuck in their limited vision, they are not getting beyond the letter of the law and a rather superficial observance of it. Similarly, today we do not have to look far to find people who, while priding themselves on living the law of the fast, are merely living the law of the diet. They abstain from food for a couple of meals and that is about the extent of it.

Through Isaiah, Jehovah opens a higher vision with the query, "Is not this the fast that I have chosen?" Then He instructs His people as He answers, "to loose the bands of wickedness, to undo the heavy burdens, and to let the oppressed go free, and that ye break every yoke?" (vv. 6–7). One could easily write a book on the meaning of this passage. If you will follow out the cross references with some diligence you will come to appreciate that "the fast the Lord has chosen" is to abstain from sin, ignorance, and servitude to our own addictions, and also to deal generously with our poor and oppressed fellow sojourners. The Lord requests a level of repentance and a level of sharing our substance with others that will open the doors of salvation and exaltation in realms to come.

In the subsequent verses, 8–12, some of the most glorious promises in all of holy writ are expounded. Cloaked in imagery, phrases like, "thy light break forth as the morning," and "thine health shall spring forth speedily," refer to great and glorious states of resurrection. And there is more. Much more. Most of these supernal promises far surpass earthly financial rewards. Yet they do apply there, too, and are surely a part of the Lord's bequests.

With the opportunity for these greater blessings in mind, can we not begin to appreciate the pathos in the hearts of the General Authorities as they plead with us to wake up and obey? One such example comes from Elder L. Tom Perry, "Oh, where is our faith? Oh, how we deprive ourselves of the blessings of the Lord by not being generous in our fast-offering contributions." (*Ensign*, May 1986, p. 32.)

Generous Fast Offerings

Paying fast offerings is not actually a law separate and apart, standing on its own. Rather it is an essential part of the law of the fast. When we catch the vision of what the Lord requests and offers, as in the Isaiah passage mentioned above, we see that fast offerings are the Lord's way of caring for the poor and needy, and part of the way to sanctify His people. The Lord's anointed have advised us to be generous. President Spencer W. Kimball was explicit enough to recommend ten times the actual cost of the meals we abstain from. (CR, April 1974, p. 184.) The admonition to be generous without having to be commanded in all things leaves it up to each one of us to decide. Herein lies not obligation but opportunity. Seize it.

> And now behold, my beloved brethren, I say unto you, do not suppose that this is all; for after ye have done all these things, if ye turn away the needy, and the naked, and visit not the sick and afflicted, and impart of your substance, if ye have, to those who stand in need—I say unto you, if ye do not any of these things, behold, your prayer is vain, and availeth you nothing, and ye are as hypocrites who do deny the faith (Alma 34:28).

"The Tithing of My People"

Whereas fast offerings are an opportunity, the payment of tithes is an obligation—a debt we discharge before the Lord. Yet it is an obligation with such significant spiritual and temporal promises that the terms *debt* and *obligation* are euphemisms. Since I have offered my thoughts on tithing already in a previous chapter, I will mention it here in respectful brevity. Have not our inspired leaders been amply explicit on the law of tithing and its appended blessings? I add only one brief example in passing. President Ezra Taft Benson implied that through our faithful observance of this law—the paying of our obligation to the Lord—our ability to retire our other debts and obligations will be enhanced: "Let us pay first our obligations to our

Heavenly Father. Then we will more easily pay our debts to our fellowmen." (*So Shall Ye Reap* [Salt Lake City: Deseret Book, 1960], p. 219.)

In summary, may I say that my purpose has not been to be comprehensive—to list every law related to financial prosperity. My intent is to cast light upon the subject in hopes of inspiring you. I urge you to pursue your own understanding of God's laws and keep seeking. As we sing in one of the hymns of Zion, "There is no end to virtue; there is no end to might; there is no end to wisdom; there is no end to light" (W. W. Phelps, "If You Could Hie to Kolob," *Hymns*, no. 284).

Practicing the laws and principles given in this book will enable you to receive greater things and be instructed by the Spirit.

THE LAW OF GIVING

The final words I leave with you are centered on the great law of giving. Like all other eternal laws, it manifests itself in degrees. In commenting on this law, I will be discreetly more explicit. Luke records a beautiful expression of the Lord: "Give, and it shall be given unto you; good measure, pressed down, and shaken together, and running over, shall men give into your bosom. For with the same measure that ye mete withal it shall be measured to you again." (Luke 6:38.)

The Lord has spoken it and you may therefore count on it more surely than the earth spinning on its axis. For at some point the heavens and the earth as we know them will pass away, but the Lord's "word shall not pass away, but shall all be fulfilled" (D&C 1:38). One cannot give without receiving abundance in return. One cannot even give obedience without being compensated by the Lord (see Mosiah 2:21–24). President Marion G. Romney said: "May I remind you that you cannot give yourself poor in this work; you can only give yourself rich. I have satisfied myself regarding the truthfulness of the statement made to me by Elder Melvin J. Ballard as he set me apart for my mission in 1920: 'A person cannot give a crust to the Lord without receiving a loaf in return.'" (*Ensign*, November 1980, p. 93.)

With this blessed law in mind, let me insert this passage from the revelation known as the "olive leaf" (D&C 88) because of the peace-producing truths it contains:

> All kingdoms have a law given;
>
> And there are many kingdoms; for there is no space in the which there is no kingdom; and there is no kingdom in which there is no space, either a greater or a lesser kingdom.
>
> And unto every kingdom is given a law; and unto every law there are certain bounds also and conditions.
>
> All beings who abide not in those conditions are not justified.
>
> For intelligence cleaveth unto intelligence; wisdom receiveth wisdom; truth embraceth truth; virtue loveth virtue; light cleaveth unto light; mercy hath compassion on mercy and claimeth her own; justice continueth its course and claimeth its own; judgment goeth before the face of him who sitteth upon the throne and governeth and executeth all things. (D&C 88:36–40.)

From this incredibly plain and precious passage we learn that our inheritance in worlds to come is based on law. More expressly, we select our kingdom to come by the level or degree of law that we live here and now.

THREE DEGREES OF THE LAW OF GIVING

1. Giving Un-anonymously

People who give service, goods, kind deeds, or money out in the open do well and accomplish much good. Without question, those who give money with their name attached have benefited others. Hundreds of thousands of students, for example, have been able to obtain an education because of generous grants from individuals and foundations that have been set up in the names of prosperous donors. I wish to take nothing away from such generosity. They will in no wise lose their reward. Yet, there is a higher law.

2. *Giving Anonymously*

In the Sermon on the Mount, the Lord contrasts the lesser law with the higher law, pointing the way to sanctification. Notice how he extends the law of giving to a nobler plane:

> Take heed that ye do not your alms before men, to be seen of them: otherwise ye have no reward of your Father which is in heaven.
>
> Therefore when thou doest thine alms, do not sound a trumpet before thee, as the hypocrites do in the synagogues and in the streets, that they may have glory of men. Verily I say unto you, They have their reward.
>
> But when thou doest alms, let not thy left hand know what thy right hand doeth:
>
> That thine alms may be in secret: and thy Father which seeth in secret himself shall reward thee openly." (Matthew 6:1–4.)

Greater than giving in one's own name is giving anonymously. People who give out of the pure joy of giving, with no other motive than love, have grown more Christlike, for that is the way He gives. He does not want compensation. He gives because giving flows out of His vast love. It is a superior way to live, and when we even begin to approach that type of giving it pleases Him.

One other reason why anonymous giving is pleasing to the Lord is that it does not create dependants, nor does it violate major premises in the great plan of salvation. Let me explain. Throughout nature the Lord teaches a significant precept: Living things are strengthened by struggle. We learned this law as children. One day while walking home from school we encountered a caterpillar that was inching its way along the sidewalk. Scooping it up on a stick, we placed the stick and our wonderful discovery into a bottle and punched holes in the top.

The next day we took the jar to school for "Show-and-Tell." Then the teacher let us in on something even more amazing. She explained that the caterpillar was going to change from its present unattractive state to one of God's most glorious creatures, an adult butterfly. (Can you see the eternal parallels in this natural symbol? All things testify of Christ and the Plan.) We were told to feed the caterpillar fresh leaves because it would have a ravenous appetite for a while, and we did. Eventually, as the teacher had described, the caterpillar spun a cocoon. Though the organism looked dead and lifeless, that stage was only temporary. In actuality, the caterpillar was not dead; it was only preparing for its new birth as a completely transformed entity. We waited almost breathlessly for the day of the emergence to come.

Finally the great day arrived and we saw the cocoon crack and shake and contort. The butterfly was breaking forth into its new life! We were so excited that we wanted it to occur all at once. But our teacher intervened, offering stern words of caution. "Do *not* help the butterfly out of its cocoon," the teacher warned. "You must let nature have its way. The butterfly gains strength through this struggle. Without the struggle the butterfly will not be. You must be wise and restrain your help." Some of us heeded the teacher and we witnessed the miracle. Some of us did not, because we wanted to "be good to the butterfly" and we "helped" when we should have withheld. Oh, what a metaphor! How plainly He teaches us!

There is, my friend, a fine art to giving and bestowing alms. There are nearly as many laws and principles in the dispensing of money as there are in obtaining it. One of the tricky passages we must negotiate in mortality has to do with giving and assisting others with the wealth Father gives to us. He is not pleased when we create dependants. No one is served when we do—not the recipient, not the giver, not the Giver.

You do no one a favor by robbing them of standing on their own legs and walking under their own power. That, too, is an ancient law. Often, loving parents cripple their children in the way they bestow their money on their offspring. Anything you keep doing for your children, you get to keep doing for your children.

The same thing can happen with people outside your family circle. It is wonderful to assist them in a time of need, but you must be careful not to intervene too early, too often, or with too much. The answer is anonymity. When you bestow gifts of money on others anonymously you can do it whenever you feel prompted, in any amount, to whomever. There are no implied obligations, and those you help can not become dependent on you. You are free to give and still free after you give. And so are they.

You will also discover something else. Your joy will be greater. That will be all the reward you could wish for, but it has been my observation that it does not stop there. The principle "You cannot give the Lord a crust without receiving a loaf in return" will invariably come into effect. You will feel inexplicable joy when you hear someone thank someone else, far greater joy than when they thank you. It may be the single biggest wealth-producing thing you ever learn to do, and I am definitely not talking about money here.

Prove it yourself. Stay alert and attentive. It will not take more than a day or two before you will hear of someone in your neighborhood or ward who is struggling with some heavy financial difficulty. Not letting your left hand know what your right is doing, so to speak, take some cash and put it in an envelope. No return address. It is even wonderful when you can mail it from another zip code or city so there is no way the gift can be traced back to you. Take my word for it, if you have not done this already, right there you will experience an inner glow of approval that is hard to describe.

But it will not end there. Sooner or later you will be in some setting, perhaps a testimony meeting, and you will hear that person stand up and tell of a miracle. He or she will describe how heart-felt prayers were answered, sometimes in the darkest hour. And you will hear him or her praise *the Lord!* Your joy will overflow because you had a chance to play a small role. Beyond that, you will have the most profound sense of gratitude that they are *not* thanking you. You will be far happier that they are praising and thanking the generous and gracious Lord on high, because you will know that to Him, and Him alone, should all the praise and thanks be given.

3. Giving Yourself to the Lord

When we give as I have described above, we are not truly giving at all. We are only redistributing. That which we give is not our own, for "the earth is the Lord's and the fulness thereof" (Psalms 24:1). Yet there is one thing that is uniquely ours and that can be given, and that one thing was never more clearly described by one of the Brethren than in a conference address by Elder Neal A. Maxwell in 1995: "The submission of one's will is really the only uniquely personal thing we have to place on God's altar. The many other things we "give," brothers and sisters, are actually the things He has already given or loaned to us. However, when you and I finally submit ourselves, by letting our individual wills be swallowed up in God's will, then we are really giving something to Him! It is the only possession which is truly ours to give!" (*Ensign*, November 1995, p. 24.)

I believe it is precisely this awesome moment of total consecration to which the Lord was pointing when he taught his Nephite disciples the following: "Therefore, if ye shall come unto me, or shall desire to come unto me, and rememberest that thy brother hath aught against thee—go thy way unto thy brother, and first be reconciled to thy brother, and then come unto me with full purpose of heart, and I will receive you" (3 Nephi 12:23).

In so many words He is saying, "When, my children, you come before me to place your all on my altar . . ." Then notice this huge key—a celestial stipulation. He says, "and rememberest that thy brother hath aught against thee." He did not say "If you have aught against your brother." He is not talking about how others show up on your ledger. This is about how you show up on theirs. "If that be the case, then before you can proceed with your offering to me, you must perform one other task," the Lord is saying. "And that task is to make a complete reconciliation with your brother. Until you have fulfilled that obligation you are not free to be giving your whole soul unto me."

One of the spiritual ramifications of freeing yourself from debt now looms spiritually immense. If you have debts, if you have financial loans in place, those with whom you are contracted have a legal lien upon you. Your soul is encumbered. When you have unpaid obligations, justice demands that you repay those loans. You are not free until you do. If you owe your brother money—if he has "aught against thee"—the Lord cannot accept your freewill offering because it is not free. Rather *you* are not free. You are bound by your word, justly and fairly, to another person. You must, therefore, reconcile yourself to your brother—keep your word, pay what is owed, and be debt free—in order to offer a total and complete consecration.

And of that occurrence, in sublimely simple words the Lord declares: "Go thy way unto thy brother, and first be reconciled to thy brother, and then come unto me with full purpose of heart, and I will receive you" (3 Nephi 12:23).

When we have fulfilled our obligation, kept our word, and paid every penny according to our previous agreements, then are we free. Then, if we choose to put our all on an altar before the Lord, it is ours to give. And, He says explicitly, when we do that—when we come unto him with *full purpose* of heart—then, in a glorious acceptance, He will receive us.

Appendix A

Inflation at 3%

(A)	Cost of Living in Today's Dollars (C)									
	$25,000	$30,000	$35,000	$40,000	$50,000	$60,000	$70,000	$80,000	$90,000	$100,000
5	$29,000	$34,800	$40,600	$46,400	$58,000	$69,600	$81,200	$92,800	$104,400	$116,000
6	$29,750	$35,700	$41,650	$47,600	$59,500	$71,400	$83,300	$95,200	$107,100	$119,000
7	$30,750	$36,900	$43,050	$49,200	$61,500	$73,800	$86,100	$98,400	$110,700	$123,000
8	$31,750	$38,100	$44,450	$50,800	$63,500	$76,200	$88,900	$101,600	$114,300	$127,000
9	$32,500	$39,000	$45,500	$52,000	$65,000	$78,000	$91,000	$104,000	$117,000	$130,000
10	$33,500	$40,200	$46,900	$53,600	$67,000	$80,400	$93,800	$107,200	$120,600	$134,000
11	$34,500	$41,400	$48,300	$55,200	$69,000	$82,800	$96,600	$110,400	$124,200	$138,000
12	$35,750	$42,900	$50,050	$57,200	$71,500	$85,800	$100,100	$114,400	$128,700	$143,000
13	$36,750	$44,100	$51,450	$58,800	$73,500	$88,200	$102,900	$117,600	$132,300	$147,000
14	$37,750	$45,300	$52,850	$60,400	$75,500	$90,600	$105,700	$120,800	$135,900	$151,000
15	$39,000	$46,800	$54,600	$62,400	$78,000	$93,600	$109,200	$124,800	$140,400	$156,000
16	$40,000	$48,000	$56,000	$64,000	$80,000	$96,000	$112,000	$128,000	$144,000	$160,000
17	$41,250	$49,500	$57,750	$66,000	$82,500	$99,000	$115,500	$132,000	$148,500	$165,000
18	$42,500	$51,000	$59,500	$68,000	$85,000	$102,000	$119,000	$136,000	$153,000	$170,000
19	$43,750	$52,500	$61,250	$70,000	$87,500	$105,000	$122,500	$140,000	$157,500	$175,000
20	$45,000	$54,000	$63,000	$72,000	$90,000	$108,000	$126,000	$144,000	$162,000	$180,000
21	$46,500	$55,800	$65,100	$74,400	$93,000	$111,600	$130,200	$148,800	$167,400	$186,000
22	$47,750	$57,300	$66,850	$76,400	$95,500	$114,600	$133,700	$152,800	$171,900	$191,000
23	$49,250	$59,100	$68,950	$78,800	$98,500	$118,200	$137,900	$157,600	$177,300	$197,000
24	$50,750	$60,900	$71,050	$81,200	$101,500	$121,800	$142,100	$162,400	$182,700	$203,000
25	$52,250	$62,700	$73,150	$83,600	$104,500	$125,400	$146,300	$167,200	$188,100	$209,000
26	$54,000	$64,800	$75,600	$86,400	$108,000	$129,600	$151,200	$172,800	$194,400	$216,000
27	$55,500	$66,600	$77,700	$88,800	$111,000	$133,200	$155,400	$177,600	$199,800	$222,000
28	$57,250	$68,700	$80,150	$91,600	$114,500	$137,400	$160,300	$183,200	$206,100	$229,000
29	$59,000	$70,800	$82,600	$94,400	$118,000	$141,600	$165,200	$188,800	$212,400	$236,000
30	$60,750	$72,900	$85,050	$97,200	$121,500	$145,800	$170,100	$194,400	$218,700	$243,000
35	$70,250	$84,300	$98,350	$112,400	$140,500	$168,600	$196,700	$224,800	$252,900	$281,000
40	$81,500	$97,800	$114,100	$130,400	$163,000	$195,600	$228,200	$260,800	$293,400	$326,000
45	$94,500	$113,400	$132,300	$151,200	$189,000	$226,800	$264,600	$302,400	$340,200	$378,000
50	$109,500	$131,400	$153,300	$175,200	$219,000	$262,800	$306,600	$350,400	$394,200	$438,000

INFLATION AT 4%

(A)	Cost of Living in Today's Dollars (C)									
	$25,000	$30,000	$35,000	$40,000	$50,000	$60,000	$70,000	$80,000	$90,000	$100,000
5	$30,500	$36,600	$42,700	$48,800	$61,000	$73,200	$85,400	$97,600	$109,800	$122,000
6	$31,750	$38,100	$44,450	$50,800	$63,500	$76,200	$88,900	$101,600	$114,300	$127,000
7	$33,000	$39,600	$46,200	$52,800	$66,000	$79,200	$92,400	$105,600	$118,800	$132,000
8	$34,250	$41,100	$47,950	$54,800	$68,500	$82,200	$95,900	$109,600	$123,300	$137,000
9	$35,500	$42,600	$49,700	$56,800	$71,000	$85,200	$99,400	$113,600	$127,800	$142,000
10	$37,000	$44,400	$51,800	$59,200	$74,000	$88,800	$103,600	$118,400	$133,200	$148,000
11	$38,500	$46,200	$53,900	$61,600	$77,000	$92,400	$107,800	$123,200	$138,600	$154,000
12	$40,000	$48,000	$56,000	$64,000	$80,000	$96,000	$112,000	$128,000	$144,000	$160,000
13	$41,750	$50,100	$58,450	$66,800	$83,500	$100,200	$116,900	$133,600	$150,300	$167,000
14	$43,250	$51,900	$60,550	$69,200	$86,500	$103,800	$121,100	$138,400	$155,700	$173,000
15	$45,000	$54,000	$63,000	$72,000	$90,000	$108,000	$126,000	$144,000	$162,000	$180,000
16	$46,750	$56,100	$65,450	$74,800	$93,500	$112,200	$130,900	$149,600	$168,300	$187,000
17	$48,750	$58,500	$68,250	$78,000	$97,500	$117,000	$136,500	$156,000	$175,500	$195,000
18	$50,750	$60,900	$71,050	$81,200	$101,500	$121,800	$142,100	$162,400	$182,700	$203,000
19	$52,750	$63,300	$73,850	$84,400	$105,500	$126,600	$147,700	$168,800	$189,900	$211,000
20	$54,750	$65,700	$76,650	$87,600	$109,500	$131,400	$153,300	$175,200	$197,100	$219,000
21	$57,000	$68,400	$79,800	$91,200	$114,000	$136,800	$159,600	$182,400	$205,200	$228,000
22	$59,250	$71,100	$82,950	$94,800	$118,500	$142,200	$165,900	$189,600	$213,300	$237,000
23	$61,500	$73,800	$86,100	$98,400	$123,000	$147,600	$172,200	$196,800	$221,400	$246,000
24	$64,000	$76,800	$89,600	$102,400	$128,000	$153,600	$179,200	$204,800	$230,400	$256,000
25	$66,750	$80,100	$93,450	$106,800	$133,500	$160,200	$186,900	$213,600	$240,300	$267,000
26	$69,250	$83,100	$96,950	$110,800	$138,500	$166,200	$193,900	$221,600	$249,300	$277,000
27	$72,000	$86,400	$100,800	$115,200	$144,000	$172,800	$201,600	$230,400	$259,200	$288,000
28	$75,000	$90,000	$105,000	$120,000	$150,000	$180,000	$210,000	$240,000	$270,000	$300,000
29	$78,000	$93,600	$109,200	$124,800	$156,000	$187,200	$218,400	$249,600	$280,800	$312,000
30	$81,000	$97,200	$113,400	$129,600	$162,000	$194,400	$226,800	$259,200	$291,600	$324,000
35	$98,750	$118,500	$138,250	$158,000	$197,500	$237,000	$276,500	$316,000	$355,500	$395,000
40	$120,000	$144,000	$168,000	$192,000	$240,000	$288,000	$336,000	$384,000	$432,000	$480,000
45	$146,000	$175,200	$204,400	$233,600	$292,000	$350,400	$408,800	$467,200	$525,600	$584,000
50	$177,750	$213,300	$248,850	$284,400	$355,500	$426,600	$497,700	$568,800	$639,900	$711,000

Inflation at 5%

(A)	\$25,000	\$30,000	\$35,000	\$40,000	\$50,000	\$60,000	\$70,000	\$80,000	\$90,000	\$100,000
				Cost of Living in Today's Dollars (C)						
5	\$32,000	\$38,400	\$44,800	\$51,200	\$64,000	\$76,800	\$89,600	\$102,400	\$115,200	\$128,000
6	\$33,500	\$40,200	\$46,900	\$53,600	\$67,000	\$80,400	\$93,800	\$107,200	\$120,600	\$134,000
7	\$35,250	\$42,300	\$49,350	\$56,400	\$70,500	\$84,600	\$98,700	\$112,800	\$126,900	\$141,000
8	\$37,000	\$44,400	\$51,800	\$59,200	\$74,000	\$88,800	\$103,600	\$118,400	\$133,200	\$148,000
9	\$38,750	\$46,500	\$54,250	\$62,000	\$77,500	\$93,000	\$108,500	\$124,000	\$139,500	\$155,000
10	\$40,750	\$48,900	\$57,050	\$65,200	\$81,500	\$97,800	\$114,100	\$130,400	\$146,700	\$163,000
11	\$42,750	\$51,300	\$59,850	\$68,400	\$85,500	\$102,600	\$119,700	\$136,800	\$153,900	\$171,000
12	\$45,000	\$54,000	\$63,000	\$72,000	\$90,000	\$108,000	\$126,000	\$144,000	\$162,000	\$180,000
13	\$47,250	\$56,700	\$66,150	\$75,600	\$94,500	\$113,400	\$132,300	\$151,200	\$170,100	\$189,000
14	\$49,500	\$59,400	\$69,300	\$79,200	\$99,000	\$118,800	\$138,600	\$158,400	\$178,200	\$198,000
15	\$52,000	\$62,400	\$72,800	\$83,200	\$104,000	\$124,800	\$145,600	\$166,400	\$187,200	\$208,000
16	\$54,500	\$65,400	\$76,300	\$87,200	\$109,000	\$130,800	\$152,600	\$174,400	\$196,200	\$218,000
17	\$60,250	\$72,300	\$84,350	\$96,400	\$120,500	\$144,600	\$168,700	\$192,800	\$216,900	\$241,000
18	\$63,250	\$75,900	\$88,550	\$101,200	\$126,500	\$151,800	\$177,100	\$202,400	\$227,700	\$253,000
19	\$66,250	\$79,500	\$92,750	\$106,000	\$132,500	\$159,000	\$185,500	\$212,000	\$238,500	\$265,000
20	\$69,750	\$83,700	\$97,650	\$111,600	\$139,500	\$167,400	\$195,300	\$223,200	\$251,100	\$279,000
21	\$72,500	\$87,000	\$101,500	\$116,000	\$145,000	\$174,000	\$203,000	\$232,000	\$261,000	\$290,000
22	\$73,250	\$87,900	\$102,550	\$117,200	\$146,500	\$175,800	\$205,100	\$234,400	\$263,700	\$293,000
23	\$76,750	\$92,100	\$107,450	\$122,800	\$153,500	\$184,200	\$214,900	\$245,600	\$276,300	\$307,000
24	\$80,750	\$96,900	\$113,050	\$129,200	\$161,500	\$193,800	\$226,100	\$258,400	\$290,700	\$323,000
25	\$84,750	\$101,700	\$118,650	\$135,600	\$169,500	\$203,400	\$237,300	\$271,200	\$305,100	\$339,000
26	\$89,000	\$106,800	\$124,600	\$142,400	\$178,000	\$213,600	\$249,200	\$284,800	\$320,400	\$356,000
27	\$93,250	\$111,900	\$130,550	\$149,200	\$186,500	\$223,800	\$261,100	\$298,400	\$335,700	\$373,000
28	\$98,000	\$117,600	\$137,200	\$156,800	\$196,000	\$235,200	\$274,400	\$313,600	\$352,800	\$392,000
29	\$103,000	\$123,600	\$144,200	\$164,800	\$206,000	\$247,200	\$288,400	\$329,600	\$370,800	\$412,000
30	\$108,000	\$129,600	\$151,200	\$172,800	\$216,000	\$259,200	\$302,400	\$345,600	\$388,800	\$432,000
35	\$138,000	\$165,600	\$193,200	\$220,800	\$276,000	\$331,200	\$386,400	\$441,600	\$496,800	\$552,000
40	\$176,000	\$211,200	\$246,400	\$281,600	\$352,000	\$422,400	\$492,800	\$563,200	\$633,600	\$704,000
45	\$224,750	\$269,700	\$314,650	\$359,600	\$449,500	\$539,400	\$629,300	\$719,200	\$809,100	\$899,000
50	\$286,750	\$344,100	\$401,450	\$458,800	\$573,500	\$688,200	\$802,900	\$917,600	\$1,032,300	\$1,147,000

INFLATION AT 6%

(A)	\$25,000	\$30,000	\$35,000	\$40,000	\$50,000	\$60,000	\$70,000	\$80,000	\$90,000	\$100,000
				Cost of Living in Today's Dollars (C)						
5	\$33,500	\$40,200	\$46,900	\$53,600	\$67,000	\$80,400	\$93,800	\$107,200	\$120,600	\$134,000
6	\$35,500	\$42,600	\$49,700	\$56,800	\$71,000	\$85,200	\$99,400	\$113,600	\$127,800	\$142,000
7	\$37,500	\$45,000	\$52,500	\$60,000	\$75,000	\$90,000	\$105,000	\$120,000	\$135,000	\$150,000
8	\$39,750	\$47,700	\$55,650	\$63,600	\$79,500	\$95,400	\$111,300	\$127,200	\$143,100	\$159,000
9	\$42,250	\$50,700	\$59,150	\$67,600	\$84,500	\$101,400	\$118,300	\$135,200	\$152,100	\$169,000
10	\$44,750	\$53,700	\$62,650	\$71,600	\$89,500	\$107,400	\$125,300	\$143,200	\$161,100	\$179,000
11	\$47,500	\$57,000	\$66,500	\$76,000	\$95,000	\$114,000	\$133,000	\$152,000	\$171,000	\$190,000
12	\$50,250	\$60,300	\$70,350	\$80,400	\$100,500	\$120,600	\$140,700	\$160,800	\$180,900	\$201,000
13	\$53,250	\$63,900	\$74,550	\$85,200	\$106,500	\$127,800	\$149,100	\$170,400	\$191,700	\$213,000
14	\$56,500	\$67,800	\$79,100	\$90,400	\$113,000	\$135,600	\$158,200	\$180,800	\$203,400	\$226,000
15	\$60,000	\$72,000	\$84,000	\$96,000	\$120,000	\$144,000	\$168,000	\$192,000	\$216,000	\$240,000
16	\$63,500	\$76,200	\$88,900	\$101,600	\$127,000	\$152,400	\$177,800	\$203,200	\$228,600	\$254,000
17	\$67,500	\$81,000	\$94,500	\$108,000	\$135,000	\$162,000	\$189,000	\$216,000	\$243,000	\$270,000
18	\$71,250	\$85,500	\$99,750	\$114,000	\$142,500	\$171,000	\$199,500	\$228,000	\$256,500	\$285,000
19	\$75,750	\$90,900	\$106,050	\$121,200	\$151,500	\$181,800	\$212,100	\$242,400	\$272,700	\$303,000
20	\$80,250	\$96,300	\$112,350	\$128,400	\$160,500	\$192,600	\$224,700	\$256,800	\$288,900	\$321,000
21	\$85,000	\$102,000	\$119,000	\$136,000	\$170,000	\$204,000	\$238,000	\$272,000	\$306,000	\$340,000
22	\$90,000	\$108,000	\$126,000	\$144,000	\$180,000	\$216,000	\$252,000	\$288,000	\$324,000	\$360,000
23	\$95,500	\$114,600	\$133,700	\$152,800	\$191,000	\$229,200	\$267,400	\$305,600	\$343,800	\$382,000
24	\$101,250	\$121,500	\$141,750	\$162,000	\$202,500	\$243,000	\$283,500	\$324,000	\$364,500	\$405,000
25	\$107,250	\$128,700	\$150,150	\$171,600	\$214,500	\$257,400	\$300,300	\$343,200	\$386,100	\$429,000
26	\$113,750	\$136,500	\$159,250	\$182,000	\$227,500	\$273,000	\$318,500	\$364,000	\$409,500	\$455,000
27	\$120,500	\$144,600	\$168,700	\$192,800	\$241,000	\$289,200	\$337,400	\$385,600	\$433,800	\$482,000
28	\$127,750	\$153,300	\$178,850	\$204,400	\$255,500	\$306,600	\$357,700	\$408,800	\$459,900	\$511,000
29	\$135,500	\$162,600	\$189,700	\$216,800	\$271,000	\$325,200	\$379,400	\$433,600	\$487,800	\$542,000
30	\$143,500	\$172,200	\$200,900	\$229,600	\$287,000	\$344,400	\$401,800	\$459,200	\$516,600	\$574,000
35	\$192,250	\$230,700	\$269,150	\$307,600	\$384,500	\$461,400	\$538,300	\$615,200	\$692,100	\$769,000
40	\$257,250	\$308,700	\$360,150	\$411,600	\$514,500	\$617,400	\$720,300	\$823,200	\$926,100	\$1,029,000
45	\$344,000	\$412,800	\$481,600	\$550,400	\$688,000	\$825,600	\$963,200	\$1,100,800	\$1,238,400	\$1,376,000
50	\$460,500	\$552,600	\$644,700	\$736,800	\$921,000	\$1,105,200	\$1,289,400	\$1,473,600	\$1,657,800	\$1,842,000

INFLATION AT 7%

(A)	Cost of Living in Today's Dollars (C)									
	$25,000	$30,000	$35,000	$40,000	$50,000	$60,000	$70,000	$80,000	$90,000	$100,000
5	$35,000	$42,000	$49,000	$56,000	$70,000	$84,000	$98,000	$112,000	$126,000	$140,000
6	$37,500	$45,000	$52,500	$60,000	$75,000	$90,000	$105,000	$120,000	$135,000	$150,000
7	$40,250	$48,300	$56,350	$64,400	$80,500	$96,600	$112,700	$128,800	$144,900	$161,000
8	$43,000	$51,600	$60,200	$68,800	$86,000	$103,200	$120,400	$137,600	$154,800	$172,000
9	$46,000	$55,200	$64,400	$73,600	$92,000	$110,400	$128,800	$147,200	$165,600	$184,000
10	$49,250	$59,100	$68,950	$78,800	$98,500	$118,200	$137,900	$157,600	$177,300	$197,000
11	$52,500	$63,000	$73,500	$84,000	$105,000	$126,000	$147,000	$168,000	$189,000	$210,000
12	$56,250	$67,500	$78,750	$90,000	$112,500	$135,000	$157,500	$180,000	$202,500	$225,000
13	$60,250	$72,300	$84,350	$96,400	$120,500	$144,600	$168,700	$192,800	$216,900	$241,000
14	$69,000	$82,800	$96,600	$110,400	$138,000	$165,600	$193,200	$220,800	$248,400	$276,000
15	$69,500	$83,400	$97,300	$111,200	$139,000	$166,800	$194,600	$222,400	$250,200	$278,000
16	$73,750	$88,500	$103,250	$118,000	$147,500	$177,000	$206,500	$236,000	$265,500	$295,000
17	$79,000	$94,800	$110,600	$126,400	$158,000	$189,600	$221,200	$252,800	$284,400	$316,000
18	$84,500	$101,400	$118,300	$135,200	$169,000	$202,800	$236,600	$270,400	$304,200	$338,000
19	$90,500	$108,600	$126,700	$144,800	$181,000	$217,200	$253,400	$289,600	$325,800	$362,000
20	$96,750	$116,100	$135,450	$154,800	$193,500	$232,200	$270,900	$309,600	$348,300	$387,000
21	$103,500	$124,200	$144,900	$165,600	$207,000	$248,400	$289,800	$331,200	$372,600	$414,000
22	$110,750	$132,900	$155,050	$177,200	$221,500	$265,800	$310,100	$354,400	$398,700	$443,000
23	$118,500	$142,200	$165,900	$189,600	$237,000	$284,400	$331,800	$379,200	$426,600	$474,000
24	$126,750	$152,100	$177,450	$202,800	$253,500	$304,200	$354,900	$405,600	$456,300	$507,000
25	$135,750	$162,900	$190,050	$217,200	$271,500	$325,800	$380,100	$434,400	$488,700	$543,000
26	$145,250	$174,300	$203,350	$232,400	$290,500	$348,600	$406,700	$464,800	$522,900	$581,000
27	$155,250	$186,300	$217,350	$248,400	$310,500	$372,600	$434,700	$496,800	$558,900	$621,000
28	$166,250	$199,500	$232,750	$266,000	$332,500	$399,000	$465,500	$532,000	$598,500	$665,000
29	$177,750	$213,300	$248,850	$284,400	$355,500	$426,600	$497,700	$568,800	$639,900	$711,000
30	$190,250	$228,300	$266,350	$304,400	$380,500	$456,600	$532,700	$608,800	$684,900	$761,000
35	$267,000	$320,400	$373,800	$427,200	$534,000	$640,800	$747,600	$854,400	$961,200	$1,068,000
40	$374,250	$449,100	$523,950	$598,800	$748,500	$898,200	$1,047,900	$1,197,600	$1,347,300	$1,497,000
45	$525,000	$630,000	$735,000	$840,000	$1,050,000	$1,260,000	$1,470,000	$1,680,000	$1,890,000	$2,100,000
50	$736,500	$883,800	$1,031,100	$1,178,400	$1,473,000	$1,767,600	$2,062,200	$2,356,800	$2,651,400	$2,946,000

INFLATION AT 8%

(A)				Cost of Living in Today's Dollars (C)						
	$25,000	$30,000	$35,000	$40,000	$50,000	$60,000	$70,000	$80,000	$90,000	$100,000
5	$36,750	$44,100	$51,450	$58,800	$73,500	$88,200	$102,900	$117,600	$132,300	$147,000
6	$39,750	$47,700	$55,650	$63,600	$79,500	$95,400	$111,300	$127,200	$143,100	$159,000
7	$42,750	$51,300	$59,850	$68,400	$85,500	$102,600	$119,700	$136,800	$153,900	$171,000
8	$46,250	$55,500	$64,750	$74,000	$92,500	$111,000	$129,500	$148,000	$166,500	$185,000
9	$50,000	$60,000	$70,000	$80,000	$100,000	$120,000	$140,000	$160,000	$180,000	$200,000
10	$54,000	$64,800	$75,600	$86,400	$108,000	$129,600	$151,200	$172,800	$194,400	$216,000
11	$58,250	$69,900	$81,550	$93,200	$116,500	$139,800	$163,100	$186,400	$209,700	$233,000
12	$63,000	$75,600	$88,200	$100,800	$126,000	$151,200	$176,400	$201,600	$226,800	$252,000
13	$68,000	$81,600	$95,200	$108,800	$136,000	$163,200	$190,400	$217,600	$244,800	$272,000
14	$73,500	$88,200	$102,900	$117,600	$147,000	$176,400	$205,800	$235,200	$264,600	$294,000
15	$79,250	$95,100	$110,950	$126,800	$158,500	$190,200	$221,900	$253,600	$285,300	$317,000
16	$85,750	$102,900	$120,050	$137,200	$171,500	$205,800	$240,100	$274,400	$308,700	$343,000
17	$92,500	$111,000	$129,500	$148,000	$185,000	$222,000	$259,000	$296,000	$333,000	$370,000
18	$100,000	$120,000	$140,000	$160,000	$200,000	$240,000	$280,000	$320,000	$360,000	$400,000
19	$108,000	$129,600	$151,200	$172,800	$216,000	$259,200	$302,400	$345,600	$388,800	$432,000
20	$116,500	$139,800	$163,100	$186,400	$233,000	$279,600	$326,200	$372,800	$419,400	$466,000
21	$125,750	$150,900	$176,050	$201,200	$251,500	$301,800	$352,100	$402,400	$452,700	$503,000
22	$136,000	$163,200	$190,400	$217,600	$272,000	$326,400	$380,800	$435,200	$489,600	$544,000
23	$146,750	$176,100	$205,450	$234,800	$293,500	$352,200	$410,900	$469,600	$528,300	$587,000
24	$158,500	$190,200	$221,900	$253,600	$317,000	$380,400	$443,800	$507,200	$570,600	$634,000
25	$171,250	$205,500	$239,750	$274,000	$342,500	$411,000	$479,500	$548,000	$616,500	$685,000
26	$185,000	$222,000	$259,000	$296,000	$370,000	$444,000	$518,000	$592,000	$666,000	$740,000
27	$199,750	$239,700	$279,650	$319,600	$399,500	$479,400	$559,300	$639,200	$719,100	$799,000
28	$215,750	$258,900	$302,050	$345,200	$431,500	$517,800	$604,100	$690,400	$776,700	$863,000
29	$233,000	$279,600	$326,200	$372,800	$466,000	$559,200	$652,400	$745,600	$838,800	$932,000
30	$251,500	$301,800	$352,100	$402,400	$503,000	$603,600	$704,200	$804,800	$905,400	$1,006,000
35	$369,750	$443,700	$517,650	$591,600	$739,500	$887,400	$1,035,300	$1,183,200	$1,331,100	$1,479,000
40	$543,000	$651,600	$760,200	$868,800	$1,086,000	$1,303,200	$1,520,400	$1,737,600	$1,954,800	$2,172,000
45	$798,000	$957,600	$1,117,200	$1,276,800	$1,596,000	$1,915,200	$2,234,400	$2,553,600	$2,872,800	$3,192,000
50	$1,172,500	$1,407,000	$1,641,500	$1,876,000	$2,345,000	$2,814,000	$3,283,000	$3,752,000	$4,221,000	$4,690,000

Appendix B

To gain a clear picture of how much of your freedom reservoir you have already accrued, you will multiply the total of your current savings by a computational factor obtained from the table below. This computational factor converts your current savings (in today's dollars) into future terms—your current savings in tomorrow's dollars.

Compounding Factor*

Years to Goal				RATE OF RETURN					
	4%	5%	6%	7%	8%	9%	10%	12%	14%
5	1.22	1.28	1.34	1.40	1.47	1.54	1.61	1.76	1.93
7	1.32	1.41	1.50	1.61	1.71	1.83	1.95	2.21	2.50
10	1.48	1.63	1.79	1.97	2.16	2.37	2.59	3.11	3.71
12	1.60	1.80	2.01	2.25	2.52	2.81	3.14	3.90	4.82
15	1.80	2.08	2.40	2.76	3.17	3.64	4.18	5.47	7.14
17	1.95	2.29	2.69	3.16	3.70	4.33	5.05	6.87	9.28
20	2.19	2.65	3.21	3.87	4.66	5.60	6.73	9.65	13.74
22	2.37	2.93	3.60	4.43	5.44	6.66	8.14	12.10	17.86
25	2.67	3.39	4.29	5.43	6.85	8.62	10.83	17.00	26.46
27	2.88	3.73	4.82	6.21	7.99	10.25	13.11	21.32	34.39
30	3.24	4.32	5.74	7.61	10.06	13.27	17.45	29.96	50.95
32	3.51	4.76	6.45	8.72	11.74	15.76	21.11	37.58	66.21
35	3.95	5.52	7.69	10.68	14.79	20.41	28.10	52.80	98.10
37	4.27	6.08	8.64	12.22	17.25	24.25	34.00	66.23	127.49
40	4.80	7.04	10.29	14.97	21.72	31.41	45.26	93.05	188.88
42	5.19	7.76	11.56	17.14	25.34	37.32	54.76	116.72	245.47
45	5.84	8.99	13.76	21.00	31.92	48.33	72.89	163.99	363.68

*compounded annually

Step One: Estimate Your Rate of Return

Your money is currently earning interest. What rate of interest (return) will you average over the years on the savings you currently own? You may not have your savings in one account or vehicle. In that case simply estimate a reasonable average for your slate of accounts.

Step Two: Locate Your Computational Factor

In the table to the left, first locate the column consistent with your estimated Rate of Return. Then move down the Years to Goal column until you locate the row closest to your goal. Move along the row until you intersect with the Rate of Return column. There you will have identified your Computational Factor. Please enter it on line 7 on page 72.

Example:

Here's an example: If you believe your current savings will average 8 percent and you are fifteen years from your desired freedom date, go to the "8%" column and scan down to the row for 15 Years to Goal. Your computational factor would be 3.17.

APPENDIX C

To estimate how much you will need to save in order to reach your freedom goal, use the table below. The figures are additive, so you can use a combination of rows, if necessary, to compute a reasonable estimate of your annual savings goal.

Annual Savings Goal

Savings Shortfall	YEARS TO GOAL							
	5	10	15	20	25	30	35	40
$25,000	4,095	1,569	787	436	254	152	92	56
$50,000	8,190	3,137	1,574	873	508	304	184	113
$100,000	16,380	6,275	3,147	1,746	1,017	608	369	226
$150,000	24,570	9,412	4,721	2,619	1,525	912	553	339
$200,000	32,759	12,549	6,295	3,492	2,034	1,216	738	452
$300,000	49,139	18,824	9,442	5,238	3,050	1,824	1,107	678
$500,000	81,899	31,373	15,737	8,730	5,084	3,040	1,845	1,130
$750,000	122,848	47,059	23,605	13,095	7,626	4,559	2,767	1,695
$1,000,000	163,798	62,746	31,474	17,460	10,168	6,080	3,690	2,260
$1,500,000	245,696	94,118	47,210	26,190	15,252	9,118	5,534	3,390
$2,000,000	327,596	125,492	62,948	34,920	20,336	12,160	7,380	4,520

Parameters: Tax-deferred, annual return: 8%, annual inflation: 4%

Example One:

If your Savings Shortfall (line 9 on page 72) is a nice, round $200,000 and your Years to Goal is fifteen, you simply go down the Savings Shortfall column on the far left to line $200,000. Then move horizontally to the right until you coincide with column 15. Your annual savings goal would be 6,295 dollars per year.

Example Two:

If your Savings Shortfall (line 9) is $350,000 and your Years to Goal is twenty, you will use two rows, the $50,000 line and the $300,000 line. Scanning down column 20, you would add the amount on line $50,000 (873) to the amount on line $300,000 (5,238) to estimate your annual savings goal: $873 + $5,238 = $6,111.

By now you are probably seeing how to use this table. Let me give you one final example.

Example Three:

If your Savings Shortfall (line 9) is $3,000,000 and your Years to Goal is thirty-five, you can go one of several ways to compute your estimate. You can either use the $1,000,000 row and then triple your number, or you could use the $1,500,000 row and double it. If you take the later route, you would go down the 35 to the $1,500,000 row. There you find 5,534. Double that amount to estimate your annual savings goal of $11,068.

If you like you can now enter your annual savings goal on line 10 on page 72.

INDEX

About the Author

Dennis R. Deaton, a respected leader in the field of human development, is the founder and chairman of the board of Quma Learning Systems. Dr. Deaton lectures on the university level and consults with companies, large and small, in the areas of continuous improvement, life management, money management, and human productivity.

He is the author of several audiocassette seminars, the co-author of the TimeMax Organizer, and the author of two books, *Money: An Owner's Manual* and *The Book on Mind Management*.

Dr. Deaton received his bachelor's degree from the University of Utah and graduated Cum Laude from Washington University in St. Louis with a doctoral degree.

Dennis and his wife, Susan, reside in Mesa, Arizona, and are the parents of nine.